Spring of Water International Ministries has added an option of viewing the Bible study video online. Please follow the steps listed below, register online at our website, then enter the following code.

9hTIBJ6icDakG1G

After following each step, then you can view the video part of the study guide on your computer, cell phone, or tablet.

Instruction for initial registration for viewing online Bible study video:

1) Open the browser and go to Spring of Water International Ministries website at www.sowim. org
2) Click on "Online Viewing Signup" at the top right corner of the webpage.
3) On the new page that popped up, enter your "Username", "Password", and "Email address", then click "Register".
4) You will receive a confirmation email from SOWIM. Please click on the link in the message to activate your account.
5) Go to the homepage at www.sowim.org and click "Online Viewing Login" at the top right corner of the webpage.
6) On the new page that popped up, enter your "Username" and "Password", then click "Login".
7) It will direct you to the "Online Material" page. Please enter the serial number provided in this manual inside the "Enter Code" window, then click "Submit". You would then be able to view the video you have purchased.
  * Note: This code can only be used once, it cannot be shared with other individuals. If you have any questions, please contact us at info@sowim.org.

Instruction for viewing online Bible study video with prior registration:

1) Open the browser and go to the Spring of Water International Ministries website at www. sowim.org
2) Click on "Online Viewing Login" at the top right corner of the webpage.
3) On the new page that popped up, enter your "Username" and "Password", then click "Login".
4) Once you are logged in, you will have access to all the videos in your account.

The Book of Ezra Study Guide

Writer: Vincent Shen, Susan Chen
English Translator: Esther Lee
Proofreading: Elena Ho, Stella Ho, Sophie Hung, Cheri Chan
General Editor: Susan Chen, Ching Chung
Publisher: Spring of Water International Ministries
Design: Taosheng Publishing House
Hong Kong Office: P.O. Box 20594, Johnston Rd Post Office, Wan Chai, Hong Kong
Taiwan Office: 27 Wu-Ling Road 300, North District, Hsinchu
US office: P.O. Box 5975, Irvine, CA 92616-5975, USA
Tel: HK: +852-95794944; Taiwan: +886-906918977; US: +949-5025688
Email: info@sowim.org
Website: www.sowim.org

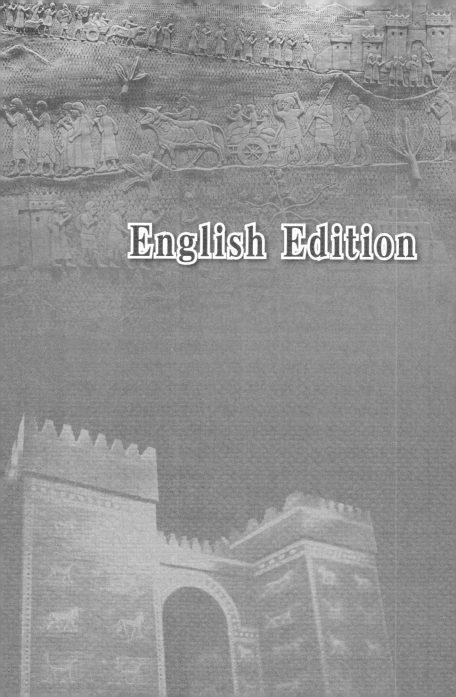

English Edition

Table of Contents
The Book of Ezra

Acknowledgment

My heart is filled with thanks for God's guidance and gracious provision in bringing the Book of Ezra Bible Study Set into publication! In the two-year production period, God has blessed us with highly respected scholars to work with us. I would like to thank the renowned Old Testament scholars, Dr. Tremper Longman III, Dr. Joseph Shao, Dr. Hing Choi Lo for sharing their scholarly insights and Dr. Justin Yang for providing the curriculum structure of the Appendix.

I am much indebted to Elder & Professor Vincent Shen. He not only teaches in the video, but also helped with the majority of the content in this study guide, including the English translation. His teachings are spiritually inspiring and insightful. Ms. Ching Chung worked side-by-side with Elder Shen, from composing the first draft of the video script to the final polishing of this study guide. This Book of Ezra Bible Study set would not exist without them.

We are blessed that Esther Lee, David Wong and Katy Lander sacrificed their personal time to do the English translation and Gilbert Yang, David Yang, and Amy Chen jointly proofread the script voluntarily. The Scriptures we use are from the New Revised Standard Version (NRSV) for English translation.

With this Book of Ezra Bible Study set, I truly believe that God will bless you to walk in the understanding of His words and to experience a vibrant spiritual life. The completion of the Book of Ezra Bible Study set with the help of all these volunteers is itself a testimony that God initiates the good work, and accomplishes His callings for the glory of His name! May God's Word prosper and His name be lifted high among His people!

Susan Chen

Founder and lifetime volunteer,
Spring of Water International Ministries (SOW)
California, USA

January, 2014

Preface

We modified the first edition of the Book of Ezra by combining the Student Study Guide and Teacher's Guide into one study guide. This Study Guide and a complementary DVD forms a Study Set. The DVD video is provided free-of-charge to our readers and supporters. They are ideal Bible learning materials for fellowship groups and adult Sunday School curriculum. In order to engage the historical and cultural context of the Old Testament, our video production team filmed the presenter's Bible teaching at the historical sites where biblical events took place. We also included significant archeological evidence and showcased artifacts from museums globally. This Bible Study Set is anything but dull or ordinary.

Our goal is to spread God's truth and equip God's people using God's Word as the foundation. By combining the Student Study Guide and the Teacher's Guide, we hope this not only eases the user's financial burden, but also offers every participant in a Bible study group the same opportunity of sharing and learning. When being used for an adult Bible education Sunday school class, this study guide can alleviate the class preparation burden so that the teacher can focus on facilitating and the class can teach themselves by studying and discussing God's word together.

Foreword

Spring of Water International Ministries Multimedia Bible Teaching Material (SMBTM) is a learning package specially made for Bible study. We designed the course based on Bible content, incorporated expert opinion from reputable Bible scholars, and dispatched professional filming teams to biblical historical sites to produce this teaching material in video and print forms. We then designed the curriculum following the "experiential and interactive" principle and "Media-based instruction" model in form. The "open learning" principle allows the teacher to break away from traditional one-way, verbal teaching. Class participation through questions and discussion are strongly encouraged here. The use of multimedia material illustrates the Bible content through presentation of archaeological findings, on-site explanation, succinct graphics and tables, and 2D/3D computer animation to inspire active participation for learning.

Although this combination may not be the only method of effective teaching, it does receive many favorable responses from Bible study groups across various study contexts. The use of SMBTM may increase Sunday school attendance, enhance learning, and sharing in small group Bible studies. Students gain deeper understanding after viewing the video. The participation in the discussion and sharing personally within the small group also contribute to the better appreciation of the Bible and its implications for everyday life.

How to use this SMBTM most effectively can be found in the Appendix section of this book.

In places where Bible teachers or ministers are lacking, this SMBTM provides high quality Bible study materials with sound theology. It has a comprehensive teaching plan for each lesson. This alleviates the burden and pressure on teachers from preparing for the Bible study class. Using SMBTM makes it easier for brothers and sisters to learn how to lead a Sunday school class or a small group Bible study. It can be brought into the mission field, as a tangible tool to train local co-workers. SMBTM can also be used as an ideal supplemental audio/video teaching material for sermons or seminary classes, rendering the history, geography, and artifacts described in the Bible visible and personable, much more than printed words alone can do.

To all our users, please feel free to adjust the teaching model suggested according to your plan and the amount of time you have. Our mission is to continue to produce more complete multimedia Bible teaching materials that can help equip churches, as well as Christian brothers and sisters elsewhere, to read, examine, and study the Bible more deeply than ever before. You may reach us at: www.sowim.org. Thank you very much!

Lesson 1
A Brief History of Israel

I. Introduction and Narrative Synopsis:

1. The Age of the Patriarchs

Human occupation can be found around the land of Israel dating back to the Stone and Bronze ages (6000-4000 B.C.). Abraham, the ancestor of the Israelites, was the father of Isaac, who was the father of Jacob. Abraham was called by God to leave the Chaldean city of Ur to settle in the land of Canaan at around 2000 B.C. (Genesis 12:1-4). God changed Jacob's name to Israel. His twelve sons were the ancestors of the twelve tribes of Israel. One of Jacob's sons, Joseph, rose to become the second most powerful man in Egypt. Joseph brought his entire extended family into Egypt during the famine. These Israelites multiplied and lived in Egypt in slavery for approximately 400 years. Finally, Moses and Joshua led them out of Egypt. They wandered in the desert for forty years, and then went across the Jordan River to settle in the land of Canaan once again.

When Joshua led the Israelites into Canaan, the Jebusites were already living in and around Jerusalem. It was a city in the Judean Mountains, between the Mediterranean Sea and the Dead Sea. The tribe of Benjamin was unable to conquer this city, so they cohabited with the Jebusites (Judges 1:21). The people of Israel formally became a nation when Saul was anointed and became the first king. Following Saul, King David reigned from 1010 to 970 B.C., and King David conquered the Jebusites making Jerusalem the capital of Israel. He built walls around the city and called it the "City of David" (II Samuel 5:6-12).

2. The First Temple Period

When Solomon, a son of David, became king, the Israelite nation was at its peak in prosperity. Solomon built the Temple for the Lord (I Kings 4:21-6:38), but his son Rehoboam was unable to hold the kingdom together. The kingdom was divided into two: the northern kingdom of Israel and the southern kingdom of Judah (I Kings 12).

The northern kingdom was conquered by the Assyrians in 722 B.C. (II Kings 17). In 586 B.C., King Nebuchadnezzar of Babylon marched into Judah and destroyed the Temple that was built by King Solomon. He captured the citizens of Judah including many of their officials and took them back to Babylon. This was the end of the southern kingdom of Judah (II Kings 25), and the end of the First Temple period.

3. The Babylonian Captivity

The city of Babylon was the capital of the Babylonian empire. This city was located in present-day Iraq, about 90 kilometers south of Baghdad. The Bible describes Babylon as a "great city" and a "mighty city" (Revelation 18:10). The Babylonian King Nebuchadnezzar conquered Jerusalem in 598 B.C., and again in 586 B.C. During his first conquest of the kingdom of Judah, the 18-year-old King Jehoiachin, who reigned for only three months, surrendered to Nebuchadnezzar together with his mother, his attendants, his nobles, and his officials. Nebuchadnezzar took all the treasures from the Temple and the royal palace. In addition to capturing tens of thousands of officials, warriors, and craftsmen, he deported all the residents of Jerusalem except for the poorest among the people of the land (II Kings 24:8-16).

Pergamon Museum in Berlin, Germany, displays a

clay tablet unearthed from the ruins of Babylon. This tablet is known as "Jehoiachin's Rations Tablet". It dated back to 595 B.C., three years after King Nebuchadnezzar's first conquest of Jerusalem. It records the food rations for Jehoiachin and his five sons, listing wheat, oil, dates, etc. The content of this tablet confirms what was recorded in the Book of Jeremiah regarding the good treatment of Jehoiachin (Jeremiah 52:31-34): "In the thirty-seventh year of the exile of King Jehoiachin of Judah, in the twelfth month, on the twenty-fifth day of the month, King Evil-merodach of Babylon, in the year he began to reign, showed favor to King Jehoiachin of Judah and brought him out of prison; he spoke kindly to him, and gave him a seat above the seats of the other kings who were with him in Babylon. So Jehoiachin put aside his prison clothes, and every day of his life he dined regularly at the king's table. For his allowance, a regular daily allowance was given him by the king of Babylon, as long as he lived, up to the day of his death."

King Nebuchadnezzar's second conquest of Jerusalem in 586 B.C. ended the dynasty of the "House of David". More people of the kingdom of Judah were taken captive and carried off to Babylon. This is known as "the Babylonian Captivity".

4. The Second Temple Period

In 539 B.C., King Cyrus of Persia attacked the Babylonian Empire and conquered it overnight. Shortly after, he started the "voluntary repatriation policy", allowing the Jews to return to Jerusalem. They rebuilt the Temple under the leadership of Zerubbabel (Ezra 1-6). Two hundred years later, in 334 B.C., Alexander the Great conquered the region and introduced Greek culture to the people who resided in the land. After Alexander died in 323 B.C., his kingdom became divided. The Land of Israel was ruled first by the Ptolemy Dynasty of Egypt, then by the Seleucid Dynasty of Syria. When Antiochus IV of the Seleucid Kingdom defiled the Temple in 175 B.C., the Israelites revolted. The rebels, led by Judas Maccabee, gained victory in 168 B.C., thus forming the second independent dynasty of Jerusalem after the House of David. They cleansed the Temple and restored the sacrifice system. Since the Maccabees came from the priestly family of Hasmoneus, this was known as the "Hasmonean Dynasty".

In 64 B.C., the Hasmonean Dynasty was defeated by the Roman general Pompey who invaded Jerusalem. The Hasmonean Dynasty came to an end. Israel did not become an independent nation again until the twentieth century. The Romans made Israel a vassal state and appointed an Edomite ruler, Herod the Great, as the client king in 37

B.C.. Herod was a great architect and builder. He renovated and expanded the Second Temple. Jesus Christ was born around 6 to 4 B.C.. He was crucified around 30-33 A.D. to save mankind. The Jewish people revolted against the Romans in 66 A.D.. By 70 A.D., the Roman general Titus destroyed the Second Temple and expelled the Jews from Jerusalem ending the Jewish revolt. This also marks the end of the Second Temple period. The Jews continued to conduct their religious activities in various synagogues throughout the land.

5. The Jewish Diaspora

In the year of 135 A.D., the Roman Emperor Hadrian sent an army to crush the second Jewish revolution. The Jews suffered an estimated 600,000 casualties. Hadrian exiled the remaining Jews from the Land of Israel and scattered them among many nations. He also changed the name of the land to Palestine (a variation of "Philistine"). This change became a source of conflict between Israelis and Palestinians which continues to this day. At the beginning of the 4th century, the Roman Emperor Constantine declared Christianity to be the official state religion of the Roman Empire. Therefore, the Romans built many churches and monasteries in Palestine in remembrance of Jesus and his disciples. Recognizing the looming threat from the east, Constantine moved the capital from Rome to Byzantium, and changed its name to 'Constantinople', which is modern-day Istanbul in Turkey. Thus the Eastern Roman Empire was also referred to as the Byzantine Empire. The Persians took Palestine in 614 A.D. and destroyed hundreds of churches. The Muslims followed and defeated Jerusalem in 638 A.D., making it one of the holiest cities for themselves, even until today. The Seljuqs from Turkey took Jerusalem in 1071 and stopped Christian pilgrims from journeying to the Holy Land. In 1095 A.D., Pope Urban II organized a Crusade and demanded the routes for pilgrimage be opened. The Crusaders took Jerusalem in 1099 A.D. and named it the "Latin State of the Near East".It was invaded by Saladin, the Sultan of Egypt. In 1187 A.D., Jerusalem was returned to Islamic rule. The Mamluks, commonly refers to Muslim slave soldiers or Muslim rulers of slave origin, ruled Egypt and Palestine for the next two and a half centuries. In 1453 A.D., Ottoman armies from its capital Bursa in Turkey, conquered Constantinople and made it to be the capital of the Ottoman Empire and changed its name to "Istanbul". In 1517 A.D., the Ottoman Empire defeated the Mamluks and expanded their territory to include Syria, Palestine, Egypt, and Northern Africa. The Ottoman Empire survived for more than four centuries. One of its Sultans, Suleiman the Magnificent, built the walls around the Old City of Jerusalem in the 16th century that still stand today.

6. Return to Zion

During World War I, Jewish scientist Dr. Chaim Weizmann contributed significantly to the British war effort. He convinced the British government that the Jews wanted to return to their homeland in Palestine. On November 2, 1917, the British government made the now famous "Balfour Declaration" stating that it would "view with favor the establishment in Palestine of a national home for the Jewish people." After the war ended in 1918, the Ottoman Empire collapsed and the League of Nations after WWI gave Great Britain the mandate to rule Palestine for 25 years.

The British Mandate for Palestine began in 1923. The local Palestinians and the returning Jews (about 11% of the population) often came in conflict and clashed. The League of Nations and Great Britain made several proposals to separate the people, but they all failed. Due to the Holocaust, when more than 6 million Jews died under Hitler from 1941 to 1945, the global community became sympathetic to the Jewish plight. With increased immigration to Palestine, Jews constituted about 33% of the population. On November 29, 1947, the United Nations passed the resolution to partition Palestine which included recommended boundaries. The city of Jerusalem was divided between Jews and Palestinian Arabs. The Jews welcomed the resolution, but the Palestinian Arabs rejected it. The British army withdrew from Palestine in April and May of 1948, as their Mandate ended.

7. Restoration of Israel

On May 14, 1948, Israel declared independence. The "Land of Palestine" was renamed the "Land of Israel". Israel was immediately attacked by the armies of the Arab League. However, the Israelite army repelled the attackers and took on more land than the UN Resolution had assigned. This war for independence generated many Palestinian refugees. In 1964, Egypt launched terrorist attacks against Israel under the assistance of Palestinian Liberation Organization. Egypt also led the armies of the United Arab Republic, which was formed in 1958, and threatened to wipe out Israel. But in June 1967, Israel launched a surprise attack against the United Arab Republic, achieving victory in only six days. The city of Jerusalem was captured by the Jews and united. This situation remains to the present day.

II. Video Viewing:

Play DVDchapter "01. Introduction".

III. Study Questions:

1. Fill in the blanks:

(1) King _____ of Israel conquered the city of the Jebusites and made it the capital of Israel. He changed its name to _____.

(2) In history, _____ was destroyed in one night, and replaced by _____; it was a great surprise that the Persian King _____ allowed the Israelites to return to Jerusalem from captivity!

(3) In the _____ Museum in Berlin, there is a clay tablet created during King Nebuchadnezzar's time. It is a record of food rations for King _____ of Judah, who was taken captive in 598 B.C., when Jerusalem was raided by the Babylonians for the first time.

2. Scripture Study:

(1) Find the Bible passages that refer to David's establishment of Jerusalem as the capital of Israel.

3. Discussion and Sharing:

(1) God promised to bless Abraham and his descendants, yet the kingdoms of Israel and Judah were both destroyed. What can we do to ensure that we properly receive God's blessings?

(2) Are there other passages in the Bible that discuss the possible exile of Israel from their promised land? Can those passages help us understand God's character and actions?

This part supplies reference for small group leaders and Sunday school teachers. If needed, please refer to Appendix: "Instruction for Small Group Leaders and Teachers". Feel free to use according to time limits and needs.

A. Preparation (5-15 minutes)

1. Ice-breaker: Conduct the following activities before starting the study:

    a. Group leader and members take turn to give brief introductions about themselves. Exchange greetings with one another.

    b. Ask group members this question: Has anyone seen pictures of the "Wailing Wall (i.e., The Western Wall)", or the "Dome of the Rock" in Jerusalem? Or, has anyone visited these places? Encourage group members to share their thoughts or experiences.

2. Introduction: After the ice breaker, the group leader gives a brief description of the Bible study program in the Multimedia Bible Teaching Materials of the Bible Study series published by Spring of Water International Ministries.

3. Opening Prayer: The group leader prays for the Holy Spirit's presence and guidance, that group members' hearts be opened, and God's Word in the Bible be the spiritual food for each, that the living water from Christ Jesus be nurturing the growth of the spiritual lives of the group leader and the members.

B. Development (40-90 minutes)

I. Overview:

The group leader gives a brief overview of the history of Israel from the beginning to the present.

II. Synopsis:

1. The Age of the Patriarchs
2. The First Temple Period
3. The Babylonian Captivity
4. The Second Temple Period

5. The Jewish Diaspora

6. Return to Zion

7. Restoration of Israel

III. Video Viewing:

Play DVD chapter "01. Introduction".

IV. Study Questions:

1. Fill in the blanks: Questions (1) - (3)

2. Scripture Study: Question (1)

3. Discussion and Sharing: Questions (1) - (2)

C. Conclusion (5-15 minutes)

1. Summary: The history of Israel speaks about the love, faithfulness, and righteousness of our God.

2. Homework Assignment:

a. Find out some information about the "Dead Sea Scroll".

b. What do we know about the Persian Empire?

 **Closing Prayer:**

Dear Heavenly Father, thank you for letting us see your faithfulness in the history of Israel. Your faithfulness is a great encouragement to me. We shall be faithful to you. In Jesus' name, we pray. Amen!

Lesson 2
Introduction to Ezra

I. Narrative Synopsis:

1. Authorship, Time, and Place

According to Jewish tradition, Ezra was the author of three books in the Bible: Chronicles, Ezra, and Nehemiah. Some scholars believe Nehemiah was the author of the book in his name, since parts of the Book of Nehemiah were written in the first-person narration. There is evidence indicating that all three books were completed around 440-430 B.C., during Ezra's lifetime, with added supplements by later authors.

Some scholars believe that the books of Ezra and Nehemiah were compiled by scribes from the non-extant books of Ezra's Biography and Memoirs of Nehemiah. They did the compilation based on themes, not necessarily in chronological order. This theme-based approach is most evident in Ezra 4:6-23, where the author inserted events after the rebuilding of the Second Temple, out of chronological order.

Although the Book of Ezra recounted a few events that occurred in Persia, it primarily recorded events that happened in Jerusalem. Since many of the narratives were written in first-person point of view, the location of the writing was likely in Jerusalem.

2. Special Features

The Book of Ezra contains several listings, including: (1) the temple vessels returned (Ezra 1:9-11); (2) the names of the repatriates in the first return from captivity (the lists in Ezra 2:3-67 are almost identical to those in Nehemiah 7:8-69); (3) the genealogy of Ezra (Ezra 7:1-5); (4) the names of the repatriates in the second return from captivity (Ezra 8:1-14); and (5) the list of people who married gentile women (Ezra 10:18-43). These lists suggest that Ezra had access to the official records. The Book of Ezra also contains seven official documents, which are: (1) the decree of Cyrus (Ezra 1:2-4); (2) Rehum's accusation (Ezra 4:11-16); (3) King Artaxerxes' reply (Ezra 4:17-22); (4) a report from Tattenai, et al. (Ezra 5:7-17);

(5) the record of King Cyrus' decree (Ezra 6:2-5); (6) King Darius' reply (Ezra 6:6-12); and (7) King Artaxerxes' authorization letter to Ezra (Ezra 7:12-26). The style of these documents is consistent with other Persian documents of that time. These official records in the Book of Ezra show that God's hand was instrumental in the return of the people and the rebuilding of all the projects. God moved the hearts of several Persian kings, eliminated many barriers, and allowed the completion of rebuilding the Temple and the city walls. However, during this process, the people of Israel showed discontentment and disobedience toward the Lord. The leaders and prophets needed to teach, monitor, and exhort the people constantly.

3. Key Verse

For Ezra had set his heart to study the law of the Lord, and to follow it, and to teach the statutes and ordinances in Israel. (Ezra 7:10)

4. Outline of the Books of Ezra and Nehemiah

- The first return period from captivity (Ezra 1-6)
- The second return period from captivity (Ezra 7-10)
- The third return period from captivity (Nehemiah 1-7)

- The revival during the Nehemiah period (Nehemiah 8-13)

5. The Decree of Cyrus

In 538 B.C., the first year of Cyrus' reign and the second year after he conquered Babylon, Persian King Cyrus wanted to win the people's hearts and to stabilize his realm. He decided to allow any foreign captives by the Chaldeans to return to their own land. He also offered that these people could take the holy vessels with them so that they could rebuild the temples of their own gods. The content of the decree, as recorded in Ezra 1:2-4, is very similar to the content of the Cyrus Cylinder, which was discovered in Babylon during the 19th century and is now kept in the British Museum in London. The cylinder recorded what Cyrus enacted: "…he has returned the holy vessels and statues taken from the temples west of the Euphrates River and the people from there. May their gods bless him…". Archaeologists also discovered other cuneiform fragments with similar messages. Apparently, the king's decree could have different versions for different peoples recorded in different languages. God moved Cyrus to issue such a decree and fulfill the prophecies made known years ago. This is the background of the first return from captivity of the Israelites.

6. The Prophecies

a. The prophecy of Isaiah

Isaiah was a Jewish prophet and taught in Jerusalem during the 7th century B.C. In Isaiah 45:1-5, he said:

"Thus says the Lord to his anointed, to Cyrus, whose right hand I have grasped to subdue nations before him and strip kings of their robes, to open doors before him — and the gates shall not be closed: I will go before you and level the mountains, I will break in pieces the doors of bronze and cut through the bars of iron, I will give you the treasures of darkness and riches hidden in secret places, so that you may know that it is I, the Lord, the God of Israel, who call you by your name. For the sake of my servant Jacob, and Israel my chosen, I call you by your name, I surname you, though you do not know me. I am the Lord, and there is no other; besides me there is no god. I arm you, though you do not know me".

Just before this passage, in Isaiah 44:28, God spoke through Isaiah:

"Who says of Cyrus, 'He is my shepherd, and he shall carry out all my purpose'; and who says of Jerusalem, 'It shall be rebuilt,' and of the temple, 'Your foundation shall be laid.'" Isaiah was moved by the Holy Spirit to foretell that Cyrus would do this, more than 200 years before the rise of the Persian Empire.

b. The prophecy of Jeremiah

Jeremiah was a prophet from the end of the 7th century B.C. to the beginning of the 6th century B.C.. After the last good king Josiah of the kingdom of Judah was killed in a battle, Jeremiah wrote the book of Lamentations. Jeremiah scolded the people for their apostasy, including offering their children as sacrifices to the foreign gods. He warned the people that disaster would come if they did not repent. In 605 B.C., he prophesied: "Therefore thus says the Lord of hosts: 'Because you have not obeyed my words, I am going to send for all the tribes of the north, says the Lord, even for King Nebuchadnezzar of Babylon, my servant, and I will bring them against this land and its inhabitants, and against all these nations around; I will utterly destroy them, and make them an object of horror and of hissing, and an everlasting disgrace. And I will banish from them the sound of mirth and the sound of gladness, the voice of the bridegroom and the voice of the bride, the sound of the millstones and the light of the lamp. This whole land shall become a ruin and a waste, and these nations shall serve the king of Babylon seventy years. Then after seventy years are completed, I will punish the king of Babylon and that nation, the land of the Chaldeans, for their iniquity,' says the Lord, 'making the land an everlasting waste.'" (Jeremiah 25:8-12)

As prophesied, King Nebuchadnezzar of Babylon conquered Jerusalem in 586 B.C., captured the king, killed the principal officers, destroyed the walls, burned the temple, took the people captive, and brought the vessels of gold and silver from the temple to Babylon. This was the end of the First Temple Period.

But God did not desert the Israelites in captivity in Babylon. He spoke through the prophet Jeremiah, "For thus says the Lord: 'Only when Babylon's seventy years are completed will I visit you, and I will fulfill to you my promise and bring you back to this place.'" (Jeremiah 29:10)

7. The Dead Sea Scrolls

There is a place called Qumran in Israel located near the northwestern shore of the Dead Sea. In the 2nd century B.C., a group of pious Jews, called the Essenes, were dissatisfied with the corruption of the religious leaders in Jerusalem. They retreated to Qumran, and lived a simple communal life there. They studied the Torah and copied scrolls of the Hebrew Scriptures. When the Romans came to suppress the Jewish revolt, the Essenes hid their scrolls in the caves around Qumran before they committed suicide, being killed, or scattered by the Roman soldiers. No one knew of the hidden scrolls for approximately 2,000 years. The scrolls were well preserved due to the arid climate in that region.

Around 1946, a Bedouin shepherd boy accidentally discovered part of the Biblical scroll collections. This started a fervent search of the scrolls in the Judean wilderness. Archaeologists found 11 caves with more than 400 complete scrolls and tens of thousands of scroll fragments. The first cave discovered by the shepherd was named Cave 1, the second Cave 2, and so on. The cave that yielded the most fragments, at more than 14,000, was Cave 4. A Norwegian scholar identified one of the fragments from Cave 4 as being a part of the Book of Nehemiah. As of today, all the books of the Old Testament Bible have been identified among the scroll fragments, except the Book of Esther. The Dead Sea Scrolls are highly regarded as one of the most influential discoveries of the twentieth century in Biblical history.

II. Video Viewing:

Play DVD chapters "02. The author and background" and "03. Outline of Ezra-Nehemiah Introduction".

III. Study Questions:

1. Fill in the blanks:

(1) In Israel, there is a place called Qumran located near the northwestern shore of the Dead Sea. In 1947, archaeologists discovered several ancient handwritten scrolls of the Bible, called _____, in the _____ near Qumran. All the scrolls were placed inside ceramicvessels. Although many of these are in fragments, scholars identified all of the Old Testament books, except _____.

(2) Toward the end of the 19th century, archaeologist Hormuzd Rassam discovered the _____ in the ruins of the city of Babylon. The inscriptions stated what King _____ enacted, that he has returned the _____ _____ of the temples and palaces west of the River Euphrates, and let the captives return to their _____ _____.

(3) The three repatriations of the Israelites from Persia happened during the reigns of _____ and _____ _____.

2. Scripture Study:

(1) Locate the Scripture references for the three returns of the Israelites from captivity.

_____

_____

_____

_____

_____

_____

_____

(2) Read I Chronicles 29:1-18 and discuss the true meaning of "offerings".

_____

_____

_____

_____

_____

_____

3. Discussion and Sharing:

(1) How does the discovery of the Dead Sea Scrolls affect our views of the Bible?

_____

_____

_____

_____

_____

_____

_____

(2) How does the discovery of the Cyrus Cylinder affect our views of God's faithfulness, power, and love?

_____

_____

_____

_____

_____

_____

_____

This part supplies reference for small group leaders and
Sunday school teachers. If needed, please refer to Appen-
dix: "Instruction for Small Group Leaders and Teachers".
Feel free to use according to time limits and needs.

A. Preparation (5-15 minutes)

1. Ice-breaker: Conduct any of the following activities
before starting the study:

    a. If there are newcomers, ask them to do short
introductions about themselves.

    b. Exchange greetings.

    c. Ask 1-3 group members to share the infor-
mation on "Dead Sea Scrolls" and the "Persian Empire" they collected in response to
Homework Assignment 1. the previous ses-
sion's assignment.

2. Introduction: After the ice-breaker, the group leader
asks the following questions:

a. Ask group members to share their impression about the Arab culture from the books or movies they have read and watched before. Have they read the story book "One Thousand and One Nights" or watched the Disney movie "Aladdin (1992)"?

b. After group members share, the group leader introduces the history of the Persian Empire in 5th century B.C., which is the background setting of the book of Ezra.

3. Opening Prayer: Pray for the presence of God and the help of Holy Spirit.

B. Development (40-90 minutes)

I. Synopsis:

1. Authorship, Time, and Place
2. Special Features
3. Key Verse
4. Outline of the books of Ezra and Nehemiah
5. The Decree of Cyrus
6. The Prophecies
7. The Dead Sea Scrolls

II. Video Viewing:

Play DVD chapters "02. The author and background" and "03. Outline of Ezra-Nehemiah Introduction".

III.Study Questions:

1. Fill in the blanks: Questions (1) - (3)
2. Scripture Study: Questions (1) - (2)
3. Discussion and Sharing: Questions (1) - (2)

C. Conclusion (5-15 minutes)

1. Summary: Recent archaeological findings bring light to the historical events in the Bible. The promise of God remains forever true to God's children.

2. Homework Assignment: Browse through the book of Ezra.

3. Closing Prayer: The group leader prays for the group and concludes the study.

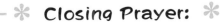

✳ Closing Prayer: ✳

Dear Heavenly Father, thank you for letting us see that you are the author of history. You can surely lead or use people whether they know you or not. Thank you for helping us know you more. Please lead us on the right path, neither deviating left or right. In Jesus' name, we pray. Amen!

Lesson 3

The First Return Period (Part 1)
Return from Babylonian Captivity
(Ezra 1:1-2:70)

I. Scripture Reading:

Ezra 1:1-2:70

II. Synopsis:

1. Responding to God's call (Ezra 1:1-11)

When King Cyrus issued the decree (Ezra 1:1-4), the people from the northern kingdom of Israel and southern kingdom of Judah had already settled in the land and raised families there. Except for the oldest among them, most people had never been to Jerusalem. Their knowledge of their homeland was limited to what they learned from the Scriptures or from stories passed down by previous generations. They did not know the current situation in Jerusalem. As a result, only those "stirred" by God (Ezra 1:5) were willing to leave their familiar environment and return to Jerusalem to rebuild the Temple, in response to God's call.

According to the Scriptures, most of the returnees were from the tribes of Judah and Benjamin (Ezra 1:5). After the death of King Solomon, Jeroboam took ten tribes and formed the Northern Kingdom of Israel. The tribes of Judah and Benjamin were still loyal to the House of David. They accepted Solomon's son Rehoboam as king and kept Jerusalem as the capital. They formed the Southern Kingdom of Judah. After Judah was destroyed by the Babylonians, those taken captive to Babylon were mostly from the tribes of Judah and Benjamin.

When God initiates a project, He provides. God moved the hearts of the friends and neighbors of those returning to Jerusalem to give them gold, silver, and valuable gifts. They also provided livestock that could be used as transportation or for food. God is so faithful that He inspired King Cyrus to instruct his treasurer to return the 5,400 articles of gold and silver that King Nebuchadnezzar took from the Temple of the Lord. Everything was given to the leader Sheshbazzar to take back to Jerusalem. Who could imagine this powerful king would do something like this? It was God himself who worked inside Cyrus' heart. The Bible says: "The king's heart is a stream of water in the hand of the Lord; he turns it wherever he will" (Proverbs 21:1).

2. The List of the Returnees (Ezra 2:1-70)

The list begins with the leaders of the first return from exile, including Zerubbabel and the priest Jeshua. The "Nehemiah" mentioned in verse 2 was not the Nehemiah of the Book of Nehemiah, the cupbearer of King Artaxerxes. Neither was "Mordecai" the Mordecai of the Book of Esther, who was Esther's foster father. For additional detail, refer to the Authorship section in the Book of Esther Overview, published by Spring of Water International Ministries in 2011.

The author provides a detailed list of families (Ezra 2:3-19) and cities of where they came from (Ezra 2:20-35). Although the numbers were not high, it showed which families were represented. This list is almost the same as the list given in Nehemiah 7:6-69. It included all of the families, priests, Levites, singers, gatekeepers, and temple servants. In total, these lists counted 29,818 adult males. Including women and children, according to Ezra 2:64, "the whole assembly together was 42,360." The slight difference between this list and the one in Nehemiah 7 could be the result of changing demographics and discrepancies in the counting method. The differences in some of the names could be due to spelling variations. Since the differences are so minor, both can be trusted as official reports on the returnees.

III. Video Viewing:

Play DVD chapter "04. The first return period: 1. Return from Babylonian Captivity".

IV. Study Questions:

1. Fill in the Blanks:

(1) "Thus says King _____ of Persia: The _____, the God of heaven, has given me all the kingdoms of the earth, and he has charged me to build him a house at _____ in Judah." (Ezra 1:2)

(2) "And let all survivors, in whatever place they reside, be assisted by the people of their place with silver and _____, with _____ and with _____, besides freewill offerings for the house of God in Jerusalem." (Ezra 1:4)

(3) "The heads of the families of _____ and _____, and the priests and the Levites— everyone whose spirit God had stirred— got ready to go up and

rebuild the house of the Lord in _____ ." (Ezra 1:5)

(4) The Temple Mount we see today was built by the Roman-appointed King of Judea _____ in about 30 B.C. He wished to gain favor from the Jews and was a great builder. He expanded the _____ , which was built by the Jews returning from exile.

2. Scripture Study:

(1) Ezra 1:1 refers to the fulfilled prophecy of Jeremiah. Which prophecy is it referring to? Where's is it recorded?

(2) Why did God preserve the throne for the House of David during Jeroboam's rebellion? Where is it recorded in the Bible?

(3) Find the Scripture references linking Zerubbabel and the Lord Jesus.

3. Discussion and Sharing:

(1) If you were settled in a foreign country away from your homeland, how would you stay in touch with the events happening in your homeland?

(2) Have you ever responded to God's calling after you are stirred by the Holy Spirit? Please share your experience.

(3) Which ministry would you like to participate in at your church, fellowship group, or Bible study group? Please share your burden.

This part supplies reference for small group leaders and Sunday school teachers. If needed, please refer to Appendix: "Instruction for Small Group Leaders and Teachers". Feel free to use according to time limits and needs.

A. Preparation (5-15 minutes)

1. Ice-breaker: Conduct any of the following activities before starting the lesson.

    a. If there are newcomers, ask them to do short introductions about themselves.

    b. Exchange greetings.

    c. Ask group members this question: Have you heard from your friends or family in your hometown recently? How did you react to the news?

2. Introduction: From the sharing of one or two group members, the group leader brings the focus to the Israelites returning to their homeland, which is the main theme of this lesson.

3. Opening Prayer: The group leader prays for the Holy Spirit's presence and guidance, that our hearts be opened, and God's word in the Bible be the lamp to our feet and light to our path, leading all of us to follow our Lord Jesus Christ.

B. Development (40-90 minutes)

I. Scripture Reading:
Ezra 1:1- 2:70

II. Synopsis:
1. Responding to God's call (Ezra 1:1-11)
2. The List of the Returnees (Ezra 2:1-70)

III. Video Viewing:
Play DVD chapter "04. The first return period: 1. Return from Babylonian Captivity".

IV. Study Questions:
1. Fill in the blanks: Questions (1) - (4)
2. Scripture Study: Questions (1) - (3)
3. Discussion/Sharing: Questions (1) - (3)

C. Conclusion (5-15 minutes)

1. Summary: It is critical for us to respond positively to the calling from God. Our response matters to God's kingdom plan, especially the ultimate blessings that God has intended for us.

2. Homework Assignment: Ask group members to find an area in the church where they can volunteer as a group. For example: Cleaning the pews inside the chapel, arranging the tables and chairs in the social hall or classroom, serving tea/lemonade at the snack/lunch table, etc. (If there are more than 8 members, group leader may divide members to form more than one group, depending on the service needs.)

3. Closing Prayer: The group leader prays for the group and concludes the study.

✳ Closing Prayer: ✳

Dear Heavenly Father, help us be a witness of your light in this world. Make us a blessing for the people around us. We look forward to a spiritual revival. We pray for our country and our city, please bless us. In Jesus' name, we pray. Amen!

Lesson 4
The First Return Period (Part 2): Restoring Sacrifices; Laying the Foundation (Ezra 3:1-13)

I. Scripture Reading:

Ezra 3:1-13

II. Synopsis:

1. Building the Altar; Offering Sacrifices (Ezra 3:1-6)

Whenever the patriarch Abraham arrived at a place where God has led him to, he immediately built an altar and offered sacrifices (Genesis 12:7-8). His descendants followed this example closely. Moses wrote down specific laws for each kind of sacrifice according to God's instructions. He recorded in detail the meaning of each sacrifice, the items to be offered, and the steps taken to make the offering. He also instructed the Israelites to offer sacrifices at the dwelling place specified by God (Deuteronomy 12:5-6).

In 537 B.C., during the seventh month (the month of Tischri, around September-October in the Gregorian calendar), three months after 42,360 Jews returned to their homeland, the Jews gathered at the ruins of Temple. The first thing they wanted to do was to build an altar where they could offer sacrifices at the location where the Temple used to stand. Despite their fear of local settlers, possibly due to their small number, the Jews gathered "as one man" (Ezra 3:1) to build the altar. They offered daily sacrifices in the morning and in the evening starting from the first day of the month. They also observed the festivals. God protected them from their enemies throughout all these activities.

2. Raising Funds; Working Together (Ezra 3:7-9)

The returnees received gold, silver, and other valuable gifts from their neighbors and friends who chose to remain in Persia. Together with their own donations, these gifts enabled them to hire masons and carpenters to rebuild the Temple. Since the city of Jerusalem is situated on top of a mountain, the masons could use the stones from the local area for the rebuilding. Each stone could weigh as much as 80 tons. However, as there were no large trees in the area, the wood needed for the Temple was shipped from Lebanon. When Solomon built the First Temple 500 years ago, Israel was strong and prominent. All the neighboring countries were glad to help, and King Solomon used the royal treasury to build the Temple (I Kings 5). This time, all the labor and materials needed for the rebuilding of the Temple came from donations from the people (Ezra 2:69).

The returnees donated labor and goods generously. Under the leadership of Governor Zerubbabel and High Priest Jeshua, the construction of the Temple began during April-May of 536 B.C. Without modern tools and construction equipment, it probably required more than 20 men to move one stone from the quarry to the site, and many more people were needed to transport cedar lumber from the harbor to Jerusalem. Every step of the work was supervised by the priests to the Levites and onto the laborers.

3. Ceremony to Lay the Foundation (Ezra 3:10-13)

Laying the foundation is the most significant step in construction. Although the archaeological evidence is not conclusive, the foundation of the Second Temple was likely laid upon the existing foundation of Solomon's Temple. When this job was completed, it marked a milestone that called for celebration. In those days, celebrating activities involves the blowing of trumpets and the beating of cymbals. On that day, the priests blew trumpets and the Levites beat cymbals, giving praise to the Lord (Ezra 3:10-11). The people sang and gave great shouts of praise. The older people who had witnessed the destruction of Solomon's temple were deeply moved and wept aloud. They recognized that the foundation of the new Temple was laid down once again among the ruins (Ezra 3:12). The shouts of joy and the weeping, combined with the sound of trumpets and cymbals, were so loud that they could be heard from very far away.

Today, the remaining foundation on the Temple Mount was not the one built during Ezra's time. The modern foundation was built in 19 B.C. by Herod the Edomite, the client king appointed by the Romans, also known as "Herod the Great" by historians. Herod decided to expand the Temple and make it bigger just to win favor from the Jews. He leveled the mountain top where the Temple stood, built a platform with large stones, and expanded the size of the Temple. Herod also added many Roman-styled buildings all around.

III. Video Viewing:

Play DVD chapter "05. The first return period: 2. Restoring Sacrifices, Laying the Foundation".

IV. Study Questions:

1. Fill in the blanks:

(1) Then _____ son of Jozadak, with his fellow priests, and _____ son of Salathiel with his kin set out to build the altar of the God of Israel, to offer _____ on it, as prescribed in the law of _____ the man of God. (Ezra 3:2)

(2) "But many of the priests and _____ and heads of families, _____ people who had seen the first house on its foundations, _____ with a loud voice when they saw this house, though many _____ aloud for joy, so that the people could not distinguish the sound of the _____ from the sound of the people's _____, for the people shouted so loudly that the sound was heard far away." (Ezra 3:12-13)

(3) "When the builders laid the foundation of the temple of the Lord, _____ in their vestments were stationed to praise the Lord with trumpets, and _____, the sons of Asaph, with cymbals, according to the directions of _____ of Israel." (Ezra 3:10)

(4) It is estimated that thousands of _____ were required to build the Temple Mount. In order to strengthen the corner of the Mount, the junction of the western and southern walls, dozens of huge stones were needed. The

average weight of one of these stones is approximately _____ tons. (cf. 1 Kings 5:17)

2. Scripture Study:

(1) According to the Bible, what festivals are to be celebrated by the Israelites during the seventh month?

---

(2) Find the instructions about burnt offerings in the Bible. Why did the returnees sacrifice burnt offerings immediately after their arrival?

---

(3) Find the genealogy of Jeshua the High Priest.

3. Discussion and Sharing:

(1) In our personal lives, how do we conduct the spiritual principle of "building an altar [and] offering a sacrifice" when we arrive at a new place?

(2) For major projects within the church (e.g. church building), how should we collaborate and work "as one man"?

_____

_____

_____

_____

(3) Is it true that all projects of a church or a Christian organization should be handled by Christians exclusively? Which major project in the Old Testament involved non-believers?

_____

_____

_____

_____

_____

_____

_____

This part supplies reference for small group leaders and Sunday school teachers. If needed, please refer to Appendix: "Instruction for Small Group Leaders and Teachers". Feel free to use according to time limits and needs.

A. Preparation (5-15 minutes)

1. Ice-breaker: Conduct the following activities before staring the study:

   a. Exchange greetings.

   b. Play a game: "Guess Who is the Leader"

   - The group forms a circle, and then sit down. Choose one person and ask him/her to leave the room.

   - Assign one person in the room to be the leader. (Note: do not let the one outside the room know who is the chosen leader.)

   - The chosen leader performs some body movements and the rest of the group follow his/her exact movements. The leader may change movements from time to time.

- Then, invite the person outside back into the room and ask him/her to guess who is the chosen leader.
- If the answer is correct, the leader will give a self-introduction, telling people, 1) his/her name, 2) the place where he/she live, 3) what are his/her favorite part about the city where he/she resides, such as climate, living quality, community culture, business activities, food and restaurants, etc. And then he/she will be the next person to step outside.

  If the person guesses wrong, he/she will give a similar self-introduction as previously stated and then choose a person to be the next leader, and ask him/her to step outside the room.

2. Introduction: After playing the game, the group leader introduces the theme of this lesson:

We learn from history that our God often selects His beloved servants to be the leaders to complete His mission and to accomplish what He has determined to do.

3. Opening Prayer: The group leader prays for the class that the Holy Spirit will guide our hearts. May God's word in the Bible be the spiritual food for each, and may the living water from Christ Jesus nurture our spiritual growth.

B. Development (40-90 minutes)

I. Scripture Reading:

Ezra 3:1-13. Genesis 12:7-8, Deuteronomy 12:5-6, Ezra 2:69

II. Synopsis:

1. Building the Altar; Offering Sacrifices (Ezra 3:1-6)
2. Raising Funds; Working Together (Ezra 3:7-9)
3. Ceremony to Lay the Foundation (Ezra 3:10-13)

III. Video Viewing:

Play DVD chapter "05. The first return period: 2. Restoring Sacrifices, Laying the foundation".

IV. Study Questions:

      1. Fill in the blanks: Questions (1) - (4)

      2. Scripture Study: Questions (1) - (3)

      3. Discussion and Sharing: Questions (1) - (3)

C. Conclusion (5-15 minutes)

1. Summary: The dedication of the returnees reflects their devotion to God, which is the anchor of a Christian life. We should have our own worship altar in our daily living and seek God's grace, fellowship, as well as forgiveness of our sins.

2. Homework Assignment: Assign students to form an action plan to do a group service project after Lesson Five.

3. Closing Prayer: The group leader prays for the group and concludes the study.

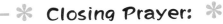

✳ Closing Prayer: ✳

Dear Heavenly Father, thank you for reminding us that we should put you first, wherever we go. We know that whenever we do something pleasing unto you, the devil might also come and harass us in our devotion. But we trust that you protect us. We believe that you will lead us away from temptation and deliver us from evil. We pray in the holy name of the Lord Jesus. Amen!

Lesson 5
The First Return Period (Parts 3 and 4) Encountering interruptions (Ezra 4:1 – 6:22)

I. Scripture Reading:

Ezra 4:1-6:22

II. Synopsis:

1. The First Return Period (Part 3) Rebuilding the Temple and Encountering Opposition (Ezra 4:1-24)

After Assyria conquered the Northern Kingdom of Israel, they exiled the local Israelites and moved the Gentiles from other territories to replace them in order prevent future rebellions. The Gentiles later intermarried with the

Israelites who were not deported and remained in the region. Since the capital of the Northern Kingdom was Samaria, these mixed-race people became known as the Samaritans. The religious practice of the Samaritans was also mixed. Then came the destruction of the Southern Kingdom of Judah by the Babylonians. Similar events happened again. "So these nations worshiped the Lord, but also served their carved images; to this day their children and their children's children continue to do as their ancestors did" (II Kings 17:41).

As the Israelites returned to their homeland, the Samaritans resented their resettlement. In Ezra 4:1, the Bible describes the Samaritans as "the adversaries of Judah and Benjamin". The Samaritans envied the blessings that the Israelites received from the Lord. When they saw that the Israelites were committed to rebuild the Temple, they attempted to join in the reconstruction. Zerubbabel, along with the other leaders of Israel, understood that the mixture of idol worshipping with serving the LORD by their ancestors was the primary reason for the destruction of the previous Temple. It was the Lord's mercy that allowed them to return to Jerusalem after many years of exile. They would not repeat the same mistakes. Therefore, they turned down the offer by the Samaritans. With their offer rejected, the Samaritans, along with other enemies of the project, were determined to obstruct the construction in any way they could.

Ezra 4:6-23 is an insert describing events that happened twenty years after the Temple foundation was initially laid (536 B.C. to 516 B.C.). It describes methods used by the enemies, such as disrupting the reconstruction of the Temple during the reign of King Artaxerxes, bribing officials, and making false accusations. Ezra 4:24 goes back to the period described in Ezra 4:5, depicting opposition during the reigns of the three previous kings of the Persian Empire: Cyrus (539 – 530 B.C.), Cambyses (530 – 522 B.C.), and Darius I (522 – 486 B.C.). Opposition to rebuild the Temple began during Cyrus' reign, and the reconstruction of the walls was opposed during the reign of Ahasuerus and again under Artaxerxes. The enemies made false accusations, claiming: "They are rebuilding that rebellious and wicked city...May it be known to the king that, if this city is rebuilt and the walls finished, they will not pay tribute, custom, or toll, and the royal revenue will be reduced" (Ezra 4:12-13). Another incident during Ahasuerus' reign was recorded in the Book of Esther. Haman, a high official for the king, almost murdered all the Jews. Details of this incident can be found in the *Book of Esther Overview - "Reversal of Fate"*, produced by Spring of Water International Ministries in year 2011.

2. The First Return Period (Part 4) Restart and Completion (Ezra 5:1-6:22)

a. The Admonition of the Prophets (Ezra 5:1-17)

In the second year of Darius I (520 B.C.), sixteen years after the Temple reconstruction was halted, God called Zechariah and Haggai to declare prophesies to the Jews (Ezra 5:1). Haggai, said to the Jews sternly: "Is it a time for you yourselves to dwell in your paneled houses, while this house lies in ruins? Now therefore thus says the Lord of hosts: Consider how you have fared. You have sown much, and harvested little. You eat, but you never have enough; you drink, but you never have your fill. You clothe yourselves, but no one is warm; and he who earns wages earn wages to put them into a bag with holes" (Haggai 1:4-6). Haggai admonished the Jews for forgetting their purpose of returning to Jerusalem. Following the interruptions to the rebuilding of the Temple, the Jews strayed from their original mission and focused on their own well-being instead. Perhaps the materials originally intended for the Temple were used to build their own houses. The prophets pointed at their failure, and galvanized them into resuming the construction of the Temple. Zerubbabel and Jeshua once again set to work at rebuilding the house of God in Jerusalem enthusiastically. (Ezra

5:2) As noted in Ezra 5:8, even the Governor of the Trans-Euphrates province, Tattenai, and his associates acknowledged "this work is being done diligently and prospers in their hands" (Ezra 5:8).

b. The Grace of God (Ezra 5:3-17)

During the time of King Darius I, new officials took over key positions in the regional government of the Trans-Euphrates province. Governor Tattenai and his associates tried to determine who was the original authority to allow the Jews in rebuilding their Temple. Although the Governor had the power to stop the project during the investigation, God's grace intervened in Tattenai's heart and he allowed the Jews to continue their work. The Bible tells us: "But the eye of their God was upon the elders of the Jews, and they did not stop them until a report reached Darius and then answer was returned by letter in reply to it." (Ezra 5:5) Haggai told the people: "'I am with you,' says the Lord." (Haggai 1:13) This is an example of God intervening on behalf of those who obey His words.

c. The Decision of King Darius (Ezra 6:1-12)

Governor Tattenai and his associates requested King Darius I to search past records in order to confirm whether or not King Cyrus had indeed made a decree authorizing the Jews to return to Jerusalem and rebuild their Temple.

King Darius I agreed and ordered the search. Government officials found a scroll in the citadel of Ecbatana in the Province of Media, which recorded the decree of Cyrus, and the contents were consistent with that of the governor's report. According to the tradition of the Medes and the Persians, decrees and edicts cannot be repealed, as what is said in Daniel 6:15, "Then the conspirators came to the king and said to him, 'Know, O king, that it is a law of the Medes and Persians that no interdict or ordinance that the king establishes can be changed.'" King Darius I not only permitted the Jews to continue the Temple reconstruction, but he also compensated the Jews for the long halt. He decreed that "the cost is to be paid to these people, in full and without delay, from the royal revenue, the tribute of the province Beyond the River." (Ezra 6:8) He also ordered that the governor would supply the bulls, rams, wheat, salt, wine, and oil needed for burnt offerings. Finally, King Darius I warned that anyone who attempted to violate these decrees would be severely punished by God and by the king. Under God's care, a potentially harmful report brought about great benefits indeed.

d. The Completion of the Temple (Ezra 6:13-22)

With the generous financial support of the government, and through the great effort of the Jews, the Temple was completed in four years. The project was finished on the 3rd day of Adar, in the 6th year of King Darius (516 B.C.), exactly 70 years after the destruction of the Temple and Jerusalem in 586 B.C. The Jews joyfully celebrated the dedication of the House of God (Ezra 6:16). These celebrations were conducted according to the Laws of Moses including offerings to the Lord and the observance of Passover. The "Second Temple", however, was not as magnificent as the First Temple built by King Solomon. Later on, it was remodelled and expanded by the Roman client King Herod the Great in 20-19 B.C. After the expansion was completed in 64 A.D., the Second Temple was much bigger than the First Temple. The Second Temple, however, was destroyed by the Roman legion when they occupied Jerusalem in 70 A.D.. Nevertheless, the Second Temple served as the center of faith for the Israelites for about 600 years, despite the many changes in government during that time.

III. Video Viewing:

Play DVD chapters "06. The First Return Period: 3. Rebuilding the Temple and the Forced Stop" and "07. The First Return Period: 4. Restart and Completion".

IV. Study Questions:

1. Fill in the blanks:

(1) "Then the people of the land _____ the people of Judah, and made them _____, and they bribed officials to frustrate their plan throughout the reign of King Cyrus of Persia and until the reign of _____ of Persia." (Ezra 4:4-5)

(2) "Then, according to the word sent by _____, Tattenai, the governor of the province Beyond the River, Shethar-bozenai, and their associates did with all diligence what King Darius had ordered. So the elders of the Jews built and prospered, through the prophesying of the prophet _____ and _____ son of Iddo. They finished their building by command of the God of Israel and by decree of _____, _____, and King _____ of Persia;" (Ezra 6:13-14)

(3) After Cyrus, the Persian Empire had four capitals: Susa, _____, _____, and _____. Ecbatana is the city of Hamadan in today's Iran.

(4) In the sixth year of King Darius' reign, which was ____ B.C., the rebuilding of the Temple was completed. It was _____ years after the destruction of the Southern Kingdom of Judah in _____ B.C., when the temple was destroyed.

2. Scripture Study:

(1) In the title of "Beyond the River" that appears in Ezra 5:3, which river does it refer to? Which areas are included in this province?

(2) How long did it take to build the First Temple? How long did it take to rebuild the Second Temple?

(3) The Book of Ezra covers events in the Persian Empire. Why does it refer Cyrus as the King of Babylon (Ezra 5:13), and Darius as the King of Assyria (Ezra 6:22)?

(4) Find prophecies in the Bible regarding the return of Jewish exiles 70 years after the fall of Jerusalem.

3. Discussion and Sharing:

(1) Have you encountered harmful rumors against you while serving the Lord? How does the narrative on the rebuilding of the Temple provide insight into your own experiences?

(2) If we truly know that God wants us to carry out a certain project, but we do not follow it, what will happen?

(3) Why does God sometimes allow the enemy to obstruct us while we are responding to his call, and faithfully carrying out His will?

(4) People sometimes say that, "If we mind His business, He minds ours". Is this view biblical?

- -

- -

- -

- -

- -

- -

- -

This part supplies reference for small group leaders and Sunday school teachers. If needed, please refer to Appendix: "Instruction for Small Group Leaders and Teachers". Feel free to use according to time limits and needs.

A. Preparation (5-15 minutes)

1. Ice-breaker: Conduct the following activities before starting the study:

  a. If there are new group members, ask them to give short introductions about themselves.

  b. Exchange greetings.

2. Introduction: After the ice breaker, the group leader does the following:

  a. Ask group members these questions: Have you experienced any major events in your study or career? Did you encounter great joy or frustration and difficulty in the process of those events?

b. Ask 1-3 group members to share their experiences. The group leader may respond and give encouragement to the group members, then move toward the content of this class.

3. Opening Prayer: Group leader prays for the presence of God and the help of the Holy Spirit.

B. Development (40-90 minutes)

I. Scripture Reading:

Ezra 4:1-6:22

II. Synopsis:

1. The First Return Period (Part 3): Rebuilding the Temple and Encountering Opposition (Ezra 4:1-24)

2. The First Return Period (Part 4): Restart and Completion (Ezra 5:1-6:22)

   a) The Admonition of the Prophets (Ezra 5:1-2)

   b) The Grace of God (Ezra 5:3-17)

   c) The Decision of King Darius (Ezra 6:1-12)

d) The Completion of the Temple (Ezra 6:13-22)

III. Video Viewing:

Play DVD chapters "05. The First Return Period: 3. Rebuilding the Temple and the Forced Stop" and "06. The First Return Period: 4. Restart and Completion".

IV. Study Questions:

1. Fill in the blanks: Questions 1-4
2. Scripture Study: Questions 1-4
3. Discussion and Sharing: Questions 1-4

C. Conclusion (5-15 minutes)

1. Summary: God allows negative circumstances or enemy's attacks against us at different time of our lives. We need to hold on to our faith and be loyal to the commission that we receive from God.

2. Homework Assignment: Encourage group members to work on their service plans from Lesson 4 and encourage them to carry it out faithfully.

3. Closing Prayer: The group leader prays for the group and concludes the study.

 Closing Prayer:

Dear heavenly Father, open our heart to care about Your business. If we have overlooked your pursuits, please send our spiritual elders and partners to remind us. Give us a teachable heart to follow the examples that we learned from the Bible. We know we are blessed under Your care. Please be with us always. We pray in Jesus' holy name. Amen!

Lesson 6

The Second Return Period (Part 1): Fasting by the River; Returning to Jerusalem (Ezra 7:1-8:36)

I. Scripture Reading:

Ezra 7:1-8:36

II. Synopsis:

1. The Hands of God (Ezra 7:1-9)

Ezra 7 records the second return of the people to Jerusalem under the leadership of Ezra during King Artaxerxes' reign (465-424 B.C.). The father of King Artaxerxes was King Ahasuerus, also called Xerxes in Greek (486-465 B.C.), and before King Xerxes was King Darius I (522-486 B.C.), who declared the support for rebuilding the Temple. The time elapsed between chapters 6 and 7 was approximately 60 years.

During these years, the Israelites faced a genocide attempt by Haman (see the Book of Esther). Although the people in Jerusalem did not serve the Lord faithfully, God was gracious and protected them nevertheless. He appointed and prepared Ezra to be the next leader. He moved the heart of the King Artaxerxes to grant "him all that he asked, for the hand of the Lord his God was upon him." (Ezra 7:6). Ezra safely led another group of people back to Jerusalem with no difficulties along the way. The scripture describes, "On the first day of the first month the journey up from Babylon was begun, and on the first day of the fifth month he came to Jerusalem, for the gracious hand of his God was upon him." (Ezra 7:9). The Lord surely led this second return.

2. Ezra, the Scribe -- A Man Prepared by God (Ezra 7:6, 10-12)

The Book of Ezra lists the genealogy of Ezra in chapter 7. He was a descendant of the high priest Aaron. The clergy of Israel was exclusively composed of Levites, and among them only the descendants of Aaron could serve as priests and religious leaders. According to the Bible, "Then the Lord spoke to Moses, saying: I hereby accept the Levites from among the Israelites as substitutes for all the firstborn that open the womb among the Israelites. The Levites shall be mine, for all the firstborn are mine; when I killed all the firstborn in the land of Egypt, I consecrated for my own all the firstborn in Israel, both human and animal; they shall be mine. I am the Lord." (Numbers 3:11-13). Ezra came from a family of priests. He was also "a scribe skilled in the law of Moses that the Lord the God of Israel had given." (Ezra 7:6). Printing presses did not exist in ancient times. The primary role of a scribe was to copy the scripture by hand. When any biblical scrolls were worn down, they would be burned and replaced by newly copied ones. Therefore, scribes were very familiar with the Bible, and were also responsible in teaching the Bible to the people.

Ezra had a good reputation for teaching the word of God. The Bible says: "For Ezra had set his heart to study the law of the Lord, and to do it, and to teach the statutes and ordinances in Israel" (Ezra 7:10). Even King Artaxerxes was aware of this. He praised Ezra as "the scribe of the law of the God of heaven" (Ezra 7:12). Ezra was very clear about his mission and his responsibilities. Not only did he excel at studying the law of God, he also followed God's word in his daily life, earning King Artaxerxes' recognition.

3. The Decree of Artaxerxes -- God's Abundant Provision (Ezra 7:13-29)

King Artaxerxes called upon Ezra to pray for blessings for the King and for his empire. Because Ezra was an expert in the Laws of God, he knew how to manage issues related to the Temple (Ezra 7:25). After commissioning a cabinet meeting with seven advisors, King Artaxerxes appointed Ezra to lead the people who wished to return to Jerusalem, including priests and Levites, to inspect the condition of Judah and Jerusalem (Ezra 7:14). They took gold, silver, bulls, and rams, along with offerings of grain and drink, as sacrifices for the altar of the Temple of the Lord. Ezra was expected to communicate the Laws of God to the people, and to appoint magistrates and judges to administer the Law (Ezra 7:14-25).

King Artaxerxes appointed Ezra to lead the Israelites in their return to Jerusalem. He and his officials also contributed gold and silver as offerings for the Lord. The King gathered all the articles originally taken from the First Temple by Nebuchadnezzar, and gave them to Ezra (Ezra 7:19). Furthermore, the King made a decree that "whatever else is required for the house of your God, which you are responsible for providing, you may provide out of the king's treasury." (Ezra 7:20) Although Ezra was indeed highly valued by the King, he knew that this favor was not a result of his own merits, but rather by the grace of God. "Blessed be the Lord, the God of our ancestors, who put such a thing as this into the heart of the king to glorify the house of the Lord in Jerusalem, and who extended to me steadfast love before the king and his counselors, and before all the king's mighty officers. I took courage, for the hand of the Lord my God was upon me, and I gathered leaders from Israel to go up with me." (Ezra 7:27-28).

4. The Wait at Ahava (Ezra 8:1-20)

Ezra received his appointment to lead the return to Jerusalem in the seventh year of King Artaxerxes' reign in 458 B.C. (Ezra 7:7). He recorded the names of individuals and families who were going to Jerusalem with him (Ezra 8:1-14). Some members of these families had already returned to Jerusalem during the first wave many years ago. This time, not counting women and small children, 1,496 adult males returned to Jerusalem.

The tribe of Levi was dedicated to serve the Lord in the Temple since Moses' time. After more than 100 years of captivity following the Temple's destruction, many Levites forgot their roles and how to perform their duties in the Temple of the Lord. They did not particularly want to return to Jerusalem. Ezra was a man of the Law, and knew in order to restore worship and sacrifices at the Temple, the Levites had to follow him back to Jerusalem. When Ezra discovered that there were no Levites among the assembly of returnees, he waited at the shore of the river at Ahava and called upon them. Finally, two families, which included 38 Levites, and 220 Temple servants, responded to Ezra's calling.

5. Returning to Jerusalem (Ezra 8:21-36)

Ezra feared God and understood His ways. This group of several thousand people, carrying a lot of valuable treasures, could be an easy target for enemies and robbers. Although he was commissioned by the king and could have requested a military escort, Ezra told the king that "the hand of our God is gracious to all who seek him, but his power and his wrath are against all who forsake him." (Ezra 8:22) Ezra relied on God for protection. He, together with all the returnees, decided to fast and pray for three days before setting out on the journey. God answered their prayers and gave them an uneventful journey. Ezra knew that returning to Jerusalem was God's will, and their safe arrival was through God's protection. He thanked God, saying, "The hand of our God was upon us, and he delivered us from the hand of the enemy and from ambushes along the way." (Ezra 8:31).

Gold and silver can be a serious temptation for anyone. Ezra handled the valuables in their possession with transparency and accountability. Before setting out for the journey, Ezra called the leading priests, the heads of the Levites and other families, to witness the weighing of gold and silver. He made a record in front of the assembly. Ezra then distributed the valuables to be carried by different people. After arriving in Jerusalem about four months later, he took the treasures, weighed and recorded them again before handing them over to the priests. Ezra was very careful in handling the treasures. This act demonstrated his character and integrity.

III. Video Viewing:

Play DVD chapter "08. The second return period: 1. Fasting by the River; Returning to Jerusalem".

IV. Study Questions:

1. Fill in the blanks:

(1) "This Ezra went up from Babylonia. He was a _____ _____ skilled in the _____ of Moses that the Lord the God of Israel had given; and the king granted him all that he asked, for _____ was upon him" (Ezra 7:6).

(2) "On the first day of the first month the journey up from

_____ was begun, and on the first day of the _____ month he came to Jerusalem, for the gracious hand of his God was upon him" (Ezra 7:9).

(3) "Blessed be the Lord, the God of our ancestors, who put such a thing as this into the heart of the king to glorify _____ in Jerusalem, and who extended to me steadfast love before the king and his counselors, and before all the king's _____. I took courage, for _____ was upon me, and I gathered leaders from Israel to go up with me" (Ezra 7:27-28).

(4) Ezra led the Israelites to return to Jerusalem for the second time in 458 B.C.. It was _____ years after the first return, which was in _____ B.C..

2. Scripture Study:

(1) Find the names of the families who participated in both returns and their numbers for both times.

(2) What percentage of the assembly during the Exodus was composed of Levites? What were their percentages in the two returns to Jerusalem?

(3) Ezra was a scribe, not a military general. The long return journey needed a lot of faith. Can you find the promises in the Bible that God will protect His children and give them victory over their enemies?

3. Discussion and Sharing:

(1) When your efforts are noticed and appreciated by your boss or superior, do you attribute the success to your

own effort, or to God's grace? Why?

(2) From the text of Ezra 7, find the qualities of Ezra that made him a leader as chosen by God.

(3) Have you ever fasted and prayed? Please give examples of fasting and praying in the Bible. What do they mean to you?

(4) When we answer God's calling and take a risk with a decision or project, how do we know God will accomplish His plan regardless of any obstacles?

Bible Study Process
for Small Group Bible Study
or Sunday School

This part supplies reference for small group leaders and Sunday school teachers. If needed, please refer to Appendix: "Instruction for Small Group Leaders and Teachers". Feel free to use according to time limits and needs.

A.Preparation (5-15 minutes)

1. **Ice-breaker:** Conduct the following activities before starting the study:
   a. Exchange greetings.
   b. Ask group members to freely share their experiences when they served at church in the previous times.

2. **Introduction:** After the ice-breaker, the Group leader responds to the sharing and leads to the content of this lesson.

3. **Opening Prayer:** Group leader prays for the presence of God and the help of the Holy Spirit.

B. Development (40-90 minutes)

I. Scripture Reading:
Ezra 7:1-8:36

II. Synopsis:
1. The Hands of God (Ezra 7:1-9)
2. Ezra, the scribe -- The Man Prepared by God (Ezra 7:6, 10-12)
3. The Decree of Artaxerxes -- God's Abundant Provision (Ezra 7:13)
4. The Wait at Ahava (Ezra 8:1-20)
5. Returning to Jerusalem (Ezra 8:21-36)

III. Video Viewing:
Play DVD chapter "07. The second return period: 1. Fasting by the River; Returning to Jerusalem".

IV. Study Questions:
1. Fill in the blanks: Questions (1) - (4)
2. Scripture Study: Questions (1) - (3)
3. Discussion and Sharing: Questions (1) - (4)

C. Conclusion (5-15 minutes)

1. Summary: Ezra sets a good example of serving God and leading God's people. Serving God is not about glorifying ourselves or having personal gain, but accomplishing God's purposes through obedience.

2. Homework Assignment: Practice a one-meal or one-day fasting prayer and ask God how you can be a testimony of the gospel? (This can be just one time practice or a weekly practice for weeks/months, depending on group member's personal choice.) Write down your prayers and check it one year later to see how God answers your prayer.

3. Closing Prayer: The group leader prays for the group members and concludes the study.

✳ Closing Prayer: ✳

Dear Heavenly Father, thank you for showing us the importance of studying the Bible, and following its teachings with faith and courage. Still, we know that we often use our own way to handle things, when we should put our trust in you. Please remind us when we go off the right path, and bring us back to it. In Jesus' name we pray. Amen!

Lesson 7

The Second Return Period (Part 2): Facing a Crisis of Faith; Restoration through Repentance and the Law (Ezra 9:1-10:44)

I. Scripture Reading:

Ezra 9:1-10:44

II. Synopsis:

1. The Crisis of Preserving their Faith (Ezra 9:1-2)

As soon as Ezra and the second group of returnees made their sin offering after their return, Ezra received a bad news about the previous group of returnees. "The people of Israel, the priests, and the Levites have not separated themselves from the peoples of the lands with their

abominations, from the Canaanites, the Hittites, the Perizzites, the Jebusites, the Ammonites, the Moabites, the
Egyptians, and the Amorites. For they have taken some of
their daughters as wives for themselves and for their sons.
Thus the holy seed has mixed itself with the peoples of the
lands, and in this faithlessness the officials and leaders
have led the way." (Ezra 9:1-2) By this time, approximately 80 years had passed since the first return led by Zerubbabel, and 60 years since the rebuilding of the Temple.
The people who returned earlier deviated from God's
word, and forgot all about the sufferings during the destruction of Judah. Most people, including their leaders,
did not remember what their ancestors experienced.

Moses taught the Israelites in Deuteronomy, saying,
"When the Lord your God brings you into the land that
you are about to enter and occupy, and he clears away
many nations before you—the Hittites, the Girgashites,
the Amorites, the Canaanites, the Perizzites, the Hivites,
and the Jebusites, seven nations mightier and more numerous than you—and when the Lord your God gives
them over to you and you defeat them, then you must utterly destroy them. Make no covenant with them and show
them no mercy. Do not intermarry with them, giving your
daughters to their sons or taking their daughters for your
sons, for that would turn away your children from following me, to serve other gods. Then the anger of the Lord

would be kindled against you, and he would destroy you quickly." (Deuteronomy 7:1-4) The nation of Israel suffered numerous times in the past because they turned away from the Lord and worshipped idols. Marriage is a very intimate relationship. After Ezra arrived in Jerusalem, he noticed that when an Israelite took a foreign wife, their children grew up with the mother's custom of worshipping foreign idols. This is not a surprise; even King Solomon, with all his wisdom, was unable to hold on to his faith after his marriage to foreign women. This brought about disasters for the Kingdom of Israel (I Kings 11:1-9). God loves the world and does not discriminate based on race. The issue here is not about race. It is about faith. The Bible tells us that Ruth and Rahab were foreign women who believed in the Lord and married Israelites. They were recognized in the family of the Israelites, and their marriages and descendants were blessed by God. Their names are listed in the genealogy of Jesus (Matthew 1:5). In fact, in Chapter 21 of Deuteronomy, Moses gave rules on marrying foreign women from regions captured in battles.

2. Ezra Repented for the People (Ezra 9:3-15)

Ezra was a loving leader. After hearing that his people did not keep the faith, he was devastated. "I tore my garment and my mantle, and pulled hair from my head and beard, and sat appalled." (Ezra 9:3) Ezra knelt before the Lord, raised his hands in prayer, and confessed on behalf of the people that needed God's mercy. Although Ezra himself did not commit the sin of marrying an idol-worshipping foreign woman, he considered himself also sinful. In his prayer, he admitted, "O my God, I am too ashamed and embarrassed to lift my face to you, my God, for our iniquities have risen higher than our heads, and our guilt has mounted up to the heavens." (Ezra 9:6) He continued with his acknowledgement of the consequences of sin. "For our iniquities we, our kings, and our priests have been handed over to the kings of the lands, to the sword, to captivity, to plundering, and to utter shame, as is now the case." (Ezra 9:7) Ezra thanked God for His grace and mercy, knowing that their punishment was lighter than what they deserved (Ezra 9:13). Finally, he repented, saying, "O Lord, God of Israel, you are just, but we have escaped as a remnant, as is now the case. Here we are before you in our guilt, though no one can face you because of this." (Ezra 9:15)

3. People's Repentance and Confession (Ezra 10:1-6)

Ezra knew that the primary reason behind the destruction of Israel and Judah was because the Israelites disobeyed and ignored their loving God. Because of grace,

God allowed them to return to their homeland. Now the people fell into the same sin again. When they saw Ezra's sorrow, they gathered around him, prayed and wept with him. The assembly displayed true repentance and contrition (Ezra 10:1). Shecaniah, son of Jehiel (this may be the same Jehiel mentioned in Ezra 10:26, who married a foreign woman) wept bitterly. He declared to Ezra that he was determined to renew his covenant with God and follow the Law. Shecaniah proposed divorcing their foreign wives and sending them away with their children. Knowing that Ezra had just arrived in Jerusalem, Jehiel offered to help, and encouraged Ezra to take courage and go through with this proposal (Ezra 10:4). Shecaniah's repentance and courageous actions touched the people, and they all swore to do what he suggested.

4. Sending Away the Foreign Wives and Children (Ezra 10:7-43)

Since this was a very important issue, Ezra, the officials, and the elders, called the returnees to assemble in front of the Temple within three days. It was raining on the day when people gathered together. They were distressed by the intermarriages, knowing that these marriage bonds represented their faithlessness. Despite mild initial opposition, the assembly followed Ezra's directions.Following Ezra's instruction, the selected heads of families took nearly three months to identify, with the assistance of elders and judges, the returnees who were married with foreign women. Many of them were priests, Levites, and temple servants. Although it was difficult for them to set aside their positions, honor, and family relationships, in the end, the returnees were all willing to repent and abide in the Laws of God. This demonstration of true repentance is precious in the eyes of God.

God hates divorce (Malachi 2:16). Why did Ezra want the Israelites to divorce their wives? Ezra had no choice but to suggest separation of the foreign wives because they not only worshipped idols, but also practiced abominable rituals from the Canaanite religions. God forbade intermarriages that led Israelites into idolatry. Ezra did not want to see the Israelites repeating the same mistakes that led to the destruction of their nation. True repentance could only be verified by heart-felt action. This is the reason why Ezra asked the Israelites to send away their idol-worshipping foreign wives and children.

III. Video Viewing:

Play DVD chapter "09. The second return period: 2. Facing a crisis of faith; Restoration through the law".

IV. Study Questions:

1. Fill in the blanks:

(1) "After these things had been done, the officials approached me and said, 'The people of Israel, the priests, and the Levites have not separated themselves from the peoples of the lands with their abominations, from the _____, the Hittites, the Perizzites, the _____ _____, the Ammonites, the _____, the Egyptians, and the Amorites. For they have taken some of their daughters as wives for themselves and for their sons. Thus the holy seed has mixed itself with the peoples of the lands, and in this faithlessness the _____ _____ and _____ have led the way'" (Ezra 9:1-2).

(2) "O Lord, God of Israel, you are _____, but we have escaped as a remnant, as is now the case. Here we are before you in our _____, though no one can face you because of this." (Ezra 9:15)

(3) "Then _____ the priest stood up and said to them, 'You have trespassed and married _____, and so increased the guilt of Israel.'" (Ezra 10:10)

(4) There was a clay tablet in the Louvre related to the month Shevat. The tablet shows that during captivity, the Jews were influenced by the local culture and adopted the

_____ calendar.

2. Scripture Study:

(1) What is the name of the prophet who served the returnees in Jerusalem at about the same time as Ezra? What
did he say about marrying foreign women?

(2) Ezra tore his tunic and cloak, pulled out his hair and
beard, and sat down appalled (Ezra 9:3). In the Old and
New Testament, can you find out other examples of similar behavior?

(3) In the practice of the Babylonians, following a divorce, children left with their mothers. Are there similar examples in the Bible?

3. Discussion and Sharing:

(1) Are marriages facing any crisis of faith today? If so, please identify it.

(2) When we see our brothers and sisters trapped in sin, what can we learn from Ezra's actions?

(3) When we see Christian brothers and sisters dating a person not yet a Christian, what can we say to them?

This part supplies reference for small group leaders and Sunday school teachers. If needed, please refer to Appendix: "Instruction for Small Group Leaders and Teachers". Feel free to use according to time limits and needs.

A. Preparation (5-15 minutes)

1. Ice-breaker: Conduct the following activities before starting the study:

    a. Exchange greetings.

    b. View Scholar's comment in DVD section 10– Dr. Tremper Longman III.

2. Introduction: After the ice-breaker, the group leader does the following:

    a. Invite 1-3 group members to share their experience of the one-day fast prayer practice.

    b. The group leader responds to the sharing and gives encouragement, then leads to the importance of prayer which is the theme of this lesson.

3. Opening Prayer: Group leader prays for the presence of God and the help of the Holy Spirit.

B. Development (40-90 minutes)

I. Scripture Reading:
Ezra 9:1-10:44

II. Synopsis:
1. The Crisis of Preserving their Faith (Ezra 9:1-2)
2. Ezra Repented for the People (Ezra 9:3-15)
3. The People's Repentance and Confession (Ezra 10:1-6)
4. Sending Away the Foreign Wives and Children (Ezra 10:7-43)

III. Video Viewing:
Play DVD chapter 9 "The second return period: 2. Facing a crisis of faith; Restoration through the law".

IV. Study Questions:

      1. Fill in the blanks: Questions (1) - (4)

      2. Scripture Study: Questions (1) - (3)

      3. Discussion and Sharing: Questions (1) - (3)

C. Conclusion (5-15 minutes)

---

1. Summary: We, as human beings, make mistakes, but God's love is never far from us when we return from our wrong doings. The most rewarding life is to dedicate our love and life to God for His worthy causes.

2. View the Scholar's comments in DVD chapter 11 and 12 – Dr. Joseph Shiao, Phillipine Bible College.

3. Closing Prayer: The group leader prays for the group and concludes the study.

✳ Closing Prayer: ✳

Dear Heavenly Father, thank you for letting us see the example set by Ezra and the repentance of the Jews during that time. Teach us to become a child after your own heart. We pray in the name of the Lord Jesus. Amen!

Suggested
Answers

Lesson 1: A Brief History of Israel

Suggested answers for your reference:

❖Fill in the blanks❖

(1) King (David) of Israel conquered the city of the Jebusites and made it the capital of Israel. He changed its name to (Jerusalem).

(2) In history, (the Kingdom of Babylon) was destroyed in one night, and replaced by (Persia); it was a great surprise that the Persian King (Cyrus) allowed the Israelites to return to Jerusalem from captivity three separate times!

(3) In the (Pergamon) Museum in Berlin, there is a clay tablet created during Nebuchadnezzar's time. It is a record of food rations for King (Jehoiachin) of Judah, who was taken captive in 598 B.C. when Jerusalem was raided by the Babylonians for the first time.

❖Scripture study❖

(1) Find the Bible passages that refer to David's establishment of Jerusalem as capital for Israel.
Suggested answer: Read 2 Samuel 5:1-12.

❖Discussion and Sharing❖

(1) God promised to bless Abraham and his descendants, yet

the kingdoms of Israel and Judah were both destroyed. What can we do to ensure that we properly receive God's blessings?

Suggested answer: The Bible tells us clearly that God loves every person in the world and His love for His children is unchanging. From the truthful record of Biblical history, we know that God's chosen people rebelled against Him, doing what was unjust and unrighteous in God's eyes: afflicting miseries on the poor and the helpless, adopting the idol worship of the pagan nations, and practicing all kinds of heinous sins and sexual immorality. Despite the fact that God had sent prophets to teach and warn them, their hearts were hardened, not willing to return to God, but taking pleasure in what they did. As a result, God allowed the fruit of their sinfulness to come to them, their country was destroyed, and they were taken captive. Learning from history, we should always have a heart yearning for God's presence and His blessings, and following His teaching and revelation by doing what is pleasing in His eyes. As we fear the Lord and serve Him alone, "only to fear the Lord your God, to walk in all his ways, to love him, to serve the Lord your God with all your heart and with all your soul" (Deuteronomy 10:12), God's blessing will not depart from us.

(2) Are there other passages in the Bible that discuss the pos-

sible exile of Israel from their promised land? Can those passages help us understand God's character and actions?

Please refer to the following passages for an understanding of the nature and character of God: Leviticus 18:28; Deuteronomy 28: 49-52; Jeremiah 5:15; Isaiah 7:18-20.

Suggested answer: Faithfulness is one aspect of God's character, affirmed throughout His word and assuring us that His will will always be accomplished. His power is so righteous that none of his foes can stand in front of Him. But when His chosen people whom he dearly loves rebel against Him, He disciplines them as described in Hebrew 12:5-7, "And you have forgotten the exhortation that addresses you as children —'My child, do not regard lightly the discipline of the Lord, or lose heart when you are punished by him; for the Lord disciplines those whom he loves, and chastises every child whom he accepts.' Endure trials for the sake of discipline. God is treating you as children; for what child is there whom a parent does not discipline?"

Although God allowed people of Israel to be driven out of their Promised Land, He miraculously re-established the sovereignty of the Jewish people over their ancient homeland after two thousand years of exile. It is prophesied in

Psalm 33:11-12, "The counsel of the Lord stands forever, the thoughts of his heart to all generations. Happy is the nation whose God is the Lord, the people whom he has chosen as his heritage." In the book of Ezra, after they were exiled from their homeland, the people of Israel remembered that God is merciful to those who love and obey Him. God also raised up leaders, three different times, to lead them back to their Promised Land.

Lesson 2: Introduction to Ezra

Suggested answers for your reference:

❖Fill in the blanks❖

(1) In Israel, there is a place called Qumran, located near the northwest shore of the Dead Sea. In 1947, archaeologists discovered several ancient handwritten scrolls of the Bible, called (The Dead Sea Scrolls), in the (11 caves) near Qumran. All the scrolls were placed inside ceramic vessels. Although many of these are in fragments, scholars were able to identify all the Old Testament books, except (Esther).

(2) Toward the end of the 19th century, archaeologist Hormuzd Rassam discovered the (Cyrus Cylinder) in the ruins of the city of Babylon. The inscriptions stated what King

(Cyrus) enacted, that he has returned the (vessels and statues) of the temples and palaces west of the River Euphrates, and let the captives return to their (own country).

(3) The three repatriations of the Israelites from Persia happened during the reigns of (Cyrus) and (Artaxerxes).

❖Scripture study❖

(1) Locate the Scripture references for the three returns of the Israelites from captivity.

Suggested answer: The first returning is recorded in Ezra 1:1-5, with the complete detailed historical record in chapters 1-6. The second return starts at Ezra 7:1-10 and is recorded in its entirety from chapter 7-10. The third return is recorded in Nehemiah 2:1-6 and the entire documentation can be found from chapters 1-7.

(2) Read I Chronicles 29:1-18 and discuss the true meaning of "offerings".

Suggested answer: This passage describes how David carefully and whole-heartedly prepared building materials for the temple, and offered a tremendous amount of his collected wealth, his motivation being "my devotion to the house of my God" (1 Chronicles 29:3), not to claim fame, nor to please people. We need to understand that the motivation of our offerings should be our love for the Lord, and caring for matters of His kingdom. Furthermore, after seeing David's example, the leaders of ancestral houses, leaders of the tribes, and the commanders of hundreds and thousands all "had given willingly" (1 Chronicles 29:9). Therefore, when we offer, we need to give willingly. In David's prayer of benediction preceding the building of the temple (1 Chronicles 29:14, 16), we understand that to be able to give for God's work is a blessing, and all we can give comes from Him. We should not take pride in ourselves.

❖Discussion and Sharing❖

(1) How does the discovery of the Dead Sea Scrolls affect my view of the Bible?

Suggested answer: As verified and confirmed by Biblical scholars, all books of the Old Testament Bible (except Esther) that we have today are almost identical with the Dead Sea Scrolls of two thousand years ago, which were discovered in the caves of Qumran. The finding demonstrates the early Christians' dedication toward God's teachings, in that they would not allow any alteration of His words. When we study the Bible today, we should possess the same attitude of fully understanding God's words, and obeying His words as we live our daily lives. Imagine the Essenes who risked their lives under the suppression of the Romans in order to preserve their copied scrolls of Biblical books. Their determination should be a historical testimony to us as the Lord's children today: how can we not treasure the Bible?

Please also refer to the explanation in the overview film for The Book of Esther produced by Spring of Water International Ministries.

(2) How does the discovery of the Cyrus Cylinder affect our views of God's faithfulness, power, and love?

Suggested answer: The scriptures of Ezra 1:2-4 are largely consistent with what was described on the Cyrus Cylinder inscribed with cuneiform script. The discovery of the Cyrus Cylinder proves the validity of Cyrus' decree.

The discovery of the Cyrus Cylinder leads us to believe that God's promise will always be accomplished, unaffected by factors of time, space, or culture. God loved His chosen people so much that He moved King Cyrus' heart to issue the repatriation policy and fulfilled the prophecies spoken through the prophets. The discovery of Biblical historical artifacts helps us to understand God's power, His everlasting love, and His unchanging faithfulness.

Lesson 3: The First Return Period (Part 1) Return from Babylonian Captivity (Ezra 1:1-2:70

Suggested answers for your reference:

❖Fill in the blanks❖

(1) Thus says King (Cyrus) of Persia: (The Lord), the God of heaven, has given me all the kingdoms of the earth, and he has charged me to build him a house at (Jerusalem) in Judah. (Ezra 1:2)

(2) In King Cyrus' decree, he asked those not returning to Jerusalem to donate (gold and silver), (goods), (and animals) to the returnees to help them rebuild the Temple. (Ezra 1:4)

(3) The heads of the families of (Judah) and (Benjamin), and the priests and the Levites—everyone whose spirit God had stirred—got ready to go up and rebuild the house of the Lord in (Jerusalem). (Ezra 1:5)

(4) The Temple Mount we see today was built by the Roman appointed King (Herod) in about 30 B.C.. He wished to gain favor from the Jews and was a great builder. He expanded the (temple), which was built by the Jews returning from exile.

❖ Scripture study ❖

(1) Ezra 1:1 refers to the fulfilled prophecies of Jeremiah. Which prophecy is it referring to? Where are they recorded?

Suggested answer: Jeremiah 25: 8-14; 29:10-14

(2) Why did God preserve the throne for the House of David during Jeroboam's rebellion? Where in the Bible is it recorded?

Suggested answer: In 2 Samuel 7:12, God says to David, "When your days are fulfilled and you lie down with your ancestors, I will raise up your offspring after you, who shall come forth from your body, and I will establish his kingdom." Our God is a faithful and merciful God. Even though King Solomon did a lot of things that displeased God, God still kept His promise to David. 1 Kings 11:28-36 provides two reasons why God did this. The first reason is recorded in v.32: "One tribe will remain his, for the sake of my servant David and for the sake of Jerusalem, the city that I have chosen out of all the tribes of Israel." The second reason is explained in v.34: "Nevertheless I will not take the whole kingdom away from him but will make him ruler all the days of his life, for the sake of my servant David whom I chose and who did keep my commandments and my statutes."

(3) Find the Scripture references linking Zerubbabel and the Lord Jesus.

Suggested answer: Zerubbabel was born during the Jew's captivity in Babylon. According to the genealogy recorded in Matthew 1:1-16, "Salathiel [was] the father of Zerubbabel." 1 Chronicles 3:17-19 has more detailed documentation: "and the sons of Jeconiah, the captive: Shealtiel his son, Malchiram, Pedaiah, Shenazzar, Jekamiah, Hoshama, and Nedabiah; The sons of Pedaiah: Zerubbabel and Shimei." Salathiel belongs to the parental generation of Zerubbabel, and Zerubbabel was the next generation of Salathiel. This is the way Jewish genealogy explains the continuity between generations. From these two genealogies, we know that Zerubbabel was the offspring of King David and also the ancestor of Joseph, the husband of Jesus' earthly mother, Mary.

❖Discussion and Sharing❖

(1) If you were settled in a foreign country away from your homeland, how would you care for the events happened in your homeland?

Suggested answer: With the advancement of technology, most of us at the present time can hear news about our homeland in real time through letters, newspapers, internet, social links (i.e., YouTube or Facebook), and friends. In the days of the ancient Persian Empire, it was very difficult for the captive Jews to hear anything about their homeland. As those who responded to the decree of King Cyrus, they cared very much about their homeland, though they were far away. With their hearts tied to their homeland, those who decided to return would give up what they had established in the foreign land to willingly offer themselves as laborers for the rebuilding of the Temple back in Jerusalem. Therefore, if God moves our heart, while living far away, we can also care about and help our homeland without being deterred by distance in time and space.

(2) Have you ever responded to God's calling after you are stirred by the Holy Spirit? Please share your experience.

Suggested answer: We are all God's children and should actively respond to God's calling; this is what we learn from the book of Ezra. We can see God's hands moving when King Cyrus issued the decree; but to respond to King Cyrus' decree meant to give up all they had. They must have struggled greatly with this decision (cf. Ezra 1:5). There was certainly unknown danger and risk to their lives and property on their journey back to Jerusalem. Despite all these, they bravely responded to God's calling. As a result, their choices were blessed by God, and their footprints were remembered in history.

(3) Which ministry would you like to participate in at your

church, fellowship group, or Bible study group? Please share your burden.

Suggested answer: During the discussion and sharing, the leader can encourage those who have not been involved in serving to participate in various ministries at church, such as setting up chairs and hymn books, or preparing drinking water. For those who are currently serving in church ministries, the leader can help them to discover their spiritual gifts, and to recognize God's calling in their lives. In order for their spiritual maturity and serving capacity to grow at the same time, it is important to serve with a joyful and humble heart together with their Christian brothers and sisters. As Paul says, when we serve, "through us spreads in every place the fragrance that comes from knowing him" (2 Corinthians 2:14). When we serve, we also need to be cautious about the consequences of envy, competitiveness, and disobedience as described in Numbers 16 regarding Korah, a Levite, and his followers in their rebellion against Moses.

Lesson 4: The First Return Period (Part 2): Restoring Sacrifices; Laying the Foundation (Ezra 3:1-13)

Suggested answers for your reference:

❖Fill in the blanks❖

(1) "Then (Jeshua) son of Jozadak, with his fellow priests, and (Zerubbabel) son of Salathiel with his kin set out to build the altar of the God of Israel, to offer (burnt offerings) on it, as prescribed in the law of (Moses) the man of God" (Ezra 3:2).

(2) "But many of the priests and (Levites) and heads of families, (old) people who had seen the first house on its foundations, (wept) with a loud voice when they saw this house, though many (shouted aloud for joy) , so that the people could not distinguish the sound of the (joyful shout) from the sound of the people's (weeping) , for the people shouted so loudly that the sound was heard far away" (Ezra 3:12-13).

(3) "When the builders laid the foundation of the temple of the Lord, the (priests) in their vestments were stationed to praise the Lord with trumpets, and the (Levites), the sons of Asaph, with cymbals, according to the directions of King (David) of Israel" (Ezra 3:10).

(4) It is estimated that thousands of (great, costly stones) were required to build the Temple Mount. In order to strengthen the corner of the Mount, the junction of the western and southern walls, dozens of huge stones were needed. The average weight of one of these stones is approximately (80) tons. (cf. 1 Kings 5:17)

❖Scripture study❖

(1) According to the Bible, what festivals are to be celebrated by the Israelites during the seventh month?

Suggested answer: According to the Bible, the important feasts and celebrations during the seventh month were the Feast of Trumpets, the Day of Atonement, and the Feast of Tabernacles. The Feast of Trumpets was on the first day of the seventh month. There are several passages in the Bible that describe this feast. For example, Leviticus 23:23-25: "The Lord spoke to Moses, saying: 'Speak to the people of Israel, saying: In the seventh month, on the first day of the month, you shall observe a day of complete rest, a holy convocation commemorated with trumpet blasts. You shall not work at your occupations; and you shall present the Lord's offering by fire.'" There is a detailed description of a burnt offering in Numbers 29:1-6: the Israelites were to prepare one young bull, one ram, and seven male lambs as a burnt offering. They were to present grain offerings, sin offerings, and drink offerings as an aroma pleasing to the

Lord, too.

The Day of Atonement was on the tenth day of the seventh month. As written in Leviticus 16:29-31: "This shall be a statute to you forever: In the seventh month, on the tenth day of the month, you shall deny yourselves, and shall do no work, neither the citizen nor the alien who resides among you. For on this day atonement shall be made for you, to cleanse you; from all your sins you shall be clean before the Lord. It is a Sabbath of complete rest to you, and you shall deny yourselves; it is a statute forever." Similarly, Leviticus 23:26-32 states that the Israelites would observe the Sabbath from the evening of the ninth day of the seventh month until the following evening.

The Feast of Tabernacles was on the fifteenth day of the seventh month and lasted for seven days, with a rest day at both the beginning and end. As written in Leviticus 23:34-37, "Speak to the people of Israel, saying: On the fifteenth day of this seventh month, and lasting seven days, there shall be the festival of booths to the Lord. The first day shall be a holy convocation; you shall not work at your occupations. Seven days you shall present the Lord's offerings by fire; on the eighth day you shall observe a holy convocation and present the Lord's offerings by fire; it is a solemn assembly; you shall not work at your occupations.

These are the appointed festivals of the Lord, which you shall celebrate as times of holy convocation, for presenting to the Lord offerings by fire—burnt-offerings and grain-offerings, sacrifices and drink-offerings, each on its proper day". During the Feast, Israelites would make booths with branches from palms and poplars and lived there for seven days as written in Leviticus 23:40-43, "On the first day you shall take the fruit of majestic trees, branches of palm trees, boughs of leafy trees, and willows of the brook; and you shall rejoice before the Lord your God for seven days. You shall keep it as a festival to the Lord seven days in the year; you shall keep it in the seventh month as a statute forever throughout your generations. You shall live in booths for seven days; all that are citizens in Israel shall live in booths, so that your generations may know that I made the people of Israel live in booths when I brought them out of the land of Egypt: I am the Lord your God."

(2) Find the instructions about burnt offerings in the Bible.
Suggested answer: As instructed in Leviticus 1:1-17, Exodus 20:24, 29:15-18, we know all the offerings, whether bull, goat, lamb, or bird, must be without defect. Their bodies would be cut to pieces and skinned, and then burned on the altar to atone for the sins of mankind. In the same way, Jesus Christ was holy and sinless; he was crucified on the cross as atonement for our sins so that our relationship

with God could be restored.

Why did the returnees sacrifice burnt offerings immediately after their arrival?

Suggested answer: When God called Moses to lead the Israelites out of Egypt, three months to the day after they left Egypt, they came to the Desert of Sinai. On the third day, the Lord descended to the top of Mount Sinai and called Moses to the top of the mountain. Moses went up. After the Lord gave Moses the Ten Commandments, He commanded that, "You shall not make gods of silver alongside me, nor shall you make for yourselves gods of gold." (Exodus 20:23) Immediately after this command, he said, "You need make for me only an altar of earth and sacrifice on it your burnt-offerings and your offerings of well-being, your sheep and your oxen; in every place where I cause my name to be remembered I will come to you and bless you." (Exodus 20:24) A further description of the burnt offering can be found in Exodus 29:42-43: "It shall be a regular burnt offering throughout your generations at the entrance of the tent of meeting before the Lord, where I will meet with you, to speak to you there. I will meet with the Israelites there, and it shall be sanctified by my glory." Therefore, after the returnees built the altar, the first offering they presented was the burnt offering. On the one hand, doing so shows that the people respected God's law; on the other hand, it expressed their desire for God's presence, that He might come to them at the altar. God favors our heart when we love Him and long for His presence. Presenting an offering is no longer just obeying the law, but expressing our love for Him. As such, the altar becomes the place where we receive His blessing.

(3) Find the genealogy of Jeshua the High Priest.

Suggested answer: Jeshua the High Priest had a genealogy of priests for all generation and they were the offspring of Aaron. As seen in Haggai 1:1 and Zechariah 6:11, he was the son of Jehozadak. 2 Kings 25:18-21 wrote about how his grandfather, Seraiah, the High Priest during Zedekiah's reign, was carried into exile when Jerusalem was destroyed and was later executed by the king of Babylon at Riblah in the land of Hamath. When Jeshua and Zerubbabel led the return of the first group of exiled Israelites to Jerusalem, rebuilt the altar, and resumed the burnt offerings, it was the first step toward the spiritual rebirth of the Israelites.

❖Discussion and Sharing❖

(1) When we arrive at a new place, how do we act out the spiritual principle of "building an altar [and] offering a sacrifice" in our personal lives?

Suggested answer: Whenever we come to a new place, for home or work, we can fulfill the spiritual principle of "building an altar and offering sacrifices" by praising the Lord for the place of home or work. We begin our days with praise, thanksgiving, and prayers, and pray for God's cleansing and protection that He will create in us "a pure heart" and "a steadfast spirit." At work, we pray for wisdom from God that we treat work as a way of worship in a broader sense: every work experience should be for God's honor.

After Abraham's death, the Philistines so envied Isaac's wealth that they stopped up all the wells dug in the time of Abraham and forced Isaac to move away (Genesis 26:14-16). Isaac moved away and dug new wells. When he discovered a well of fresh water, and the herdsmen of Gerar quarreled with Isaac's herdsmen, Isaac did not argue with them and instead chose to move away again. The way Isaac handled the dispute was pleasing to the Lord that God "appeared to him at Beersheba and said, 'I am the God of your father Abraham; do not be afraid, for I am with you and will bless you and make your offspring numerous for my servant Abraham's sake.' So he built an altar there, called on the name of the Lord" (Genesis 26:24-25). The story of Isaac building an altar is a good lesson for us when facing challenges.

A spiritual altar at home can begin with the family reading

the Bible, praying, and worshiping together. Parents should lead their kids in reading the Bible regularly, and should pray for and with their kids. We can also open our house for home fellowship as a way of worshipping God.

(2) For the major projects of the church, how should we collaborate and work "as one man"?

Suggested answer: The first step is for the pastors and the team to pray together and seek God's will. Do not rush to plan and then have God endorse your plan. The second step is to choose the workers carefully. It is essential that they all have a mature faith and dedication in loving the Lord and they can work together with their gifts and abilities, dedicated to one another. "Lead a life worthy of the calling to which you have been called, with all humility and gentleness, with patience, bearing with one another in love, making every effort to maintain the unity of the Spirit in the bond of peace. There is one body and one Spirit, just as you were called to the one hope of your calling, one Lord, one faith, one baptism, one God and Father of all, who is above all and through all and in all" (Ephesians 4:2-6).

(3) Is it true that all the projects of the church or a Christian organization should be handled by Christians exclusively? Which major project in the Old Testament can involve non-believers?

Suggested answer: The Bible tells us that when King Solomon built the temple, he used thirty-three hundred foremen to supervise the work of more than a hundreds of thousand laborers. As specified in the Bible, among these workmen, only thirty thousand were Israelites. (1 Kings 5:13) The rest of them were craftsmen of Hiram, and men of Gebal. (1 Kings 5:18) It is understandable that the building projects of the church do not necessarily have to be carried out only by Christians; the church can hire some professionals to carry out a few of the general operational tasks. While working together, Christians can use this opportunity to introduce the gospel to non-believers through their own life's testimonies. When Spring of Water International Ministries was shooting "the Book of Esther Overview" video, after working together for three weeks, our Iranian guide became interested in Christianity. Before the end of our trip, he expressed his desire to have a Bible in Persian so that he could study the Bible carefully. A few years later, he became a believer. This is a wonderful testimony.

Lesson 5:
The First Return Period (Parts 3 and 4) Encountering interruptions (Ezra 4:1 – 6:22)

Suggested answers for your reference:

❖Fill in the blanks❖

(1) "Then the people of the land (discouraged) the people of Judah, and made them (afraid to build), and they bribed officials to frustrate their plan throughout the reign of King Cyrus of Persia and until the reign of (King Darius) of Persia" (Ezra 4:4-5).

(2) "Then, according to the word sent by (King Darius), Tattenai, the governor of the province Beyond the River, Shethar-bozenai, and their associates did with all diligence what King Darius had ordered. So the elders of the Jews built and prospered, through the prophesying of the prophet (Haggai) and (Zechariah) son of Iddo. They finished their building by command of the God of Israel and by decree of (Cyrus), (Darius), and King (Artaxerxes) of Persia" (Ezra 6:13-14).

(3) After Cyrus, the Persian Empire had four capitals: Susa, (Persepolis), (Babylon), and (Ecbatona). The Ecbatana is in today's Iran, the city of Hamadan.

(4) In the sixth year of King Darius' reign, which was (516)

B.C., the rebuilding of the Temple was completed. It was (70) years after the destruction of the Southern Kingdom of Judah in (586) B.C., when the temple was destroyed.

❖Scripture study❖

(1) In the title of "Beyond the River" that appears in Ezra 5:3, which river does it refer to? Which areas are included in this province?

Suggested answer: The Trans-Euphrates is "Abarnahara" in Aramaic. Its English direct translation means "beyond the river." The judicial region that sits west to the river of Euphrates was called the Beyond the River province. This province of the Persian Empire included Syria, Samaria, and Judah. It was presided over by the governor of Trans-Euphrates.

(2) How long did it take to build the First Temple? How long did it take to build the Second Temple?

Suggested answer: According to 1 Kings 6:1, "In the fourth year of Solomon's reign over Israel, in the month of Ziv, which is the second month, he began to build the house of the Lord." And then in 1 Kings 6:37-38, the Bible says: "In the fourth year the foundation of the house of the Lord was laid, in the month of Ziv. In the eleventh year, in the month of Bul, which is the eighth month, the house was finished in all its parts, and according to all its specifications. He was *seven years* in building it."

As documented in the Book of Ezra, the construction of the second Temple resumed in the second year of King Darius after the prophets Haggai and Zechariah prophesied to the people of Judah. The project was earlier interrupted but not stopped by Tattenai, governor of Trans-Euphrates, who asked King Darius if King Cyrus did in fact issue a decree to rebuild the temple. When King Darius found the decree in the royal archives of Ecbatana, he strongly supported the rebuilding of the Lord's temple, paid out of the royal treasury for the expense of the work, and ordered the rebuilding to continue unhindered. The construction of the Second Temple was completed on the third day of the month Adar, in the sixth year of the reign of King Darius. It took *four years* to finish rebuilding the temple of the Lord. (cf. Ezra 6: 1-15)

(3) The Book of Ezra covers the events in the Persian Empire. Why does it refer to Cyrus as the King of Babylon (Ezra 5:13), and Darius as the King of Assyria (Ezra 6:22)?

Suggested answer: These titles have historical implications. The Assyrian, Babylonian, and Persian empires were founded at different times in the Mesopotamian plain. Because Cyrus conquered the Babylonian Empire and ruled over the land of Babylon, he also used the title "the King of Babylon" to assert his ruling authority over the land.

The Assyrian Empire was conquered in 612 B.C.. During its strongest period, it ruled over what would become the Persian Empire. As a result, sometimes the king of Persia was called "the king of Assyria". Therefore, the author of the Book of Ezra might have used the title, "the King of Assyria" to imply how the shame of the captivity of the Northern Kingdom was removed through the hands of the king of Persia.

(4) Find prophecies in the Bible regarding the return of Jewish exiles 70 years after the fall of Jerusalem.

Suggested answer: Through the prophecy of Jeremiah, God says, "This whole land shall become a ruin and a waste, and these nations shall serve the king of Babylon seventy years. Then after seventy years are completed, I will punish the king of Babylon and that nation, the land of the Chaldeans, for their iniquity, says the Lord, making the land an everlasting waste." (Jeremiah 25:11-12) Also in Jeremiah 29:10: "For thus says the Lord: Only when Babylon's seventy years are completed will I visit you, and I will fulfill to you my promise and bring you back to this place."

❖Discussion and Sharing❖

(1) Have you encountered harmful rumors against you while serving the Lord? How does the narrative on the rebuilding

of the Temple provide insight into your own experiences? Suggested answer: When the people of Judah returned to Jerusalem, they joyfully and willingly rebuilt the temple of the Lord. However, they encountered constant false accusations, disgrace, and destruction from their enemies. Similarly, today when we work in ministries, we can sometimes be frustrated by rumors or hurt by lies. We may feel distressed or disappointed that our goal is not reached and God's calling unfulfilled.

Similar experiences occurred in the life of Jesus. He, the only begotten Son of God, was sent to earth to redeem the world. Although He is holy and sinless, God allowed Him to face false accusation from the high priests and eventually die on a cross. It seemed that God's plan of redemption had failed, yet before his death, Jesus cried, "It is finished." (John 19:30). At that time no one knew when Jesus accepted the persecution, his death completed God's plan to redeem the world. Indeed, God had prepared Jesus' death as a sacrifice of atonement. He is now sitting at God's right hand and given sovereignty over Heaven and Earth.

Disciples in the early church were also persecuted by Jews and gentiles alike. Some were stoned, imprisoned, or even crucified. Through facing constant persecution and needing to move, churches were established everywhere, and the gospel was spread from Jerusalem to all corners of the world.

As said in 1 Peter 4:13-14, "But rejoice insofar as you are sharing Christ's sufferings, so that you may also be glad and shout for joy when his glory is revealed. If you are reviled for the name of Christ, you are blessed, because the spirit of glory, which is the Spirit of God, is resting on you." Don't be surprised if even as an honest, kind, and righteous Christian, you encounter false accusation. We should realize the truth that God allows us to experience suffering so that we will be able to enjoy His glory with Him in eternity.

(2) If we truly know that God wants us to carry out a certain project, but we do not follow it, what will happen?

Suggested answer: No one can stop God's plan. If we don't respond, God will call others to do it. Through Mordecai in Esther 4:13-14, God made it clear. "Do not think that in the king's palace you will escape any more than all the other Jews. For if you keep silence at such a time as this, relief and deliverance will rise for the Jews from another quarter, but you and your father's family will perish. Who knows? Perhaps you have come to royal dignity for just such a time as this."

It is no surprise that when we are called by Him to do something, we might refuse out of fear. In the case of Esther, she could have rejected this calling for the danger of losing her life when she approached the king without being summoned. But Mordecai said confidently that if she did not do it, God would use another way and find another person to accomplish His plan.

Often times, we hear calls for some cause but it is hard for us to give up our wealth and affection, like the wealthy young man in Mark 10. Jesus loved him and asked him to sell everything he had and give to the poor. Even though Jesus said to him that he would have treasures in heaven, it was hard for him to abandon his great wealth. The Bible tells us that although he asked to know how to inherit eternal life, in the end, "he went away grieving" because he rejected the way that Jesus instructed him (Mark 10:22). Although he held on to the wealth belonging to his transient life on earth, he lost the imperishable treasure and blessings that God had promised to him in eternity.

The prophet Jonah in the Old Testament heard God's calling for him to go to Nineveh to preach against their wickedness. Because of their evil ways and violence, Jonah did not consider them worthy of such grace. He might also worry: "Forty days more, and Nineveh shall be overthrown!" (Jonah 3:4) Jonah decided to run away from God's calling, but God gave him a lesson, that he must learn to obey and rely on God. God let him stay alive inside a great fish for three days and three nights, feeling his life ebbing away until he cried out to God in desperation, "But I with the voice of thanksgiving will sacrifice to you;

what I have vowed I will pay. Deliverance belongs to the Lord!" (Jonah 2:9) God then commanded the fish to spit Jonah onto dry land.

Later when Jonah was greatly displeased and angry with God after people in Nineveh repented, it became evident that Jonah truly did not want God to forgive and bless the people in Nineveh after their repentance. He arrogantly believed that they were enemies of Israel and did not deserve God's compassion and redemption. Through an ordinary bush, God taught Jonah to abandon his prejudice and to know the reach of God's love and mercy.

From these three examples, we find that when God calls us to do something, it is because of His love for us. The wise and most blessed decision for us is to submit to His will fully.

(3) Why does God sometimes allow the enemy to obstruct us while we are responding to his call, and faithfully carrying out His will?

Suggested answer: Jesus is the Son of God, the true God of the Trinity, and is presented by God as a sacrifice of atonement. Jesus submitted to God's plan, and was born onto the earth through the impregnation of the Holy Spirit. When he began to teach on earth, God allowed a lot of scribes of the law, Pharisees, and priests to criticize His actions, challenge His authority, and finally crucify Him with false witnesses. In the Book of Ezra, God allowed the enemies to plot against the returning Israelites. "They bribed officials to frustrate their plan throughout the reign of King Cyrus of Persia and until the reign of King Darius of Persia." (Ezra 4:5) Out of fear and despair, the people of Israel halted the building of the house of God, which they had so joyfully started.

Although fear often times paralyzes our action, and despair interrupts our momentum or calls into question our initial calling, Psalm 66:10-12 encourages us: "For you, O God, have tested us; you have tried us as silver is tried. You brought us into the net; you laid burdors on our backs; you let people ride over our heads; we went through fire and through water; yet you have brought us out to a spacious place." This passage explains one of the mysteries of God's will; that is, God aims to strengthen our faith by allowing us to face adversaries, so that we can experience His gracious deliverance and His power. Paul also said, "All things work together for good for those who love God, who are called according to his purpose." (Romans 8:28). Therefore, whenever we are attacked or obstructed by enemies, keep in mind that it is a great opportunity for us to grow and be blessed.

James 1:2-4, 12: "My brothers and sisters, whenever you face trials of any kind, consider it nothing but joy, because you know that the testing of your faith produces endurance; and let endurance have its full effect, so that you may be mature and complete, lacking in nothing. ...Blessed is anyone who endures temptation. Such a one has stood the test and will receive the crown of life that the Lord has promised to those who love him."

(4) People sometimes say that, "if we mind His business, He minds ours." Is this view Biblical?

Suggested answer: As Jesus Christ tells us in Matthew 6:33, "Strive first for the kingdom of God and his righteousness, and all these things will be given to you as well." When we mind God's business, God will provide all we need. On the other hand, if we mind only our own business, thinking we could be more satisfied when we hoard selfishly everything we have for ourselves, we most certainly will not participate in God's work and hence miss out the blessings that come with that.

In the Book of Haggai, God spoke harshly to the men of Judah through the prophet Haggai, "Is it a time for you yourselves to live in your paneled houses, while this house lies in ruins? Now therefore, thus says the Lord of hosts: Consider how you have fared. You have sown much, and harvested little; you eat, but you never have enough; you drink, but you never have your fill; you clothe yourselves, but no one is warm; and you that earn wages earn wages to put them into a bag with holes." (Haggai 1:4-6) In Philippians 2:4-5, Paul says, "Let each of you look not to your own interests, but to the interests of others. Let the same mind be in you that was in Christ Jesus."

If God, who knows our desperate inability to save ourselves from His righteous anger against our sin, has sent His own Son to save us, how much more would He care for all the other needs we have in this life? "He who did not withhold his own Son, but gave him up for all of us, will he not with him also give us everything else?" (Romans 8:32)

Lesson 6:
The Second Return Period (Part 1):
Fasting by the River; Returning to Jerusalem
(Ezra 7:1 - 8:36)

Suggested answers for your reference:

❖Fill in the blanks❖

(1) "This Ezra went up from Babylonia. He was a (scribe) skilled in the (law) of Moses that the Lord the God of Israel had given; and the king granted him all that he asked, for (the hand of the Lord his God) was upon him" (Ezra 7:6).

(2) "On the first day of the first month the journey up from (Babylon) was begun, and on the first day of the (fifth)

month he came to Jerusalem, for the gracious hand of his God was upon him" (Ezra 7:9).

(3) "Blessed be the Lord, the God of our ancestors, who put such a thing as this into the heart of the king to glorify (the house of the Lord) in Jerusalem, and who extended to me steadfast love before the king and his counselors, and before all the king's (mighty officers). I took courage, for (the hand of the Lord my God) was upon me, and I gathered leaders from Israel to go up with me" (Ezra 7:27-28).

(4) Ezra led the Israelites to return to Jerusalem for the second time in 458 B.C.. It was (79) years after the first return, which was in (537) B.C..

❖Scripture study❖

(1) Find the names of the families who participated in both returns and their numbers for both times.

(The answer can be found in Ezra 2 and 8.)

(2-a). What percentage of the assembly during the Exodus was composed of Levites?

Suggested answer: According to Numbers 26, the number of the Israelites was six hundred one thousand seven hundred thirty, before they entered the land of Canaan. Among them, the number of Levites was 23,000, which is about 3.8 percent of the total population.

(2-b). What were their percentages in the two returns to Jerusalem?

Suggested answer: In the first return to Jerusalem, the whole company numbered 42,360 people. If we add the number of women and children, there might be around 80,000-10,000 people altogether. The Levites accounted for only 74, not even one thousandth. (See Ezra 2:40.) The total number for the people of the second return was about 3,000-4,000 people and there were less than 40 Levites. (See Ezra 8:18, 19.) So the Levites accounted for about one percent of the total returnees. After 100 years of living in exile, the Levites probably did not know what they could do for the Lord, their God. They might also fear that people would not bring their sacrifices to the Lord and hence they could not make a living out of their services in the temple. That is why there were such small numbers of Levites who were willing to return to Jerusalem.

(3) Ezra was a scribe, not a military general. The long return journey needed a lot of faith. Can you find the promises in the Bible that God will protect His children and give them victory over their enemies?

Suggested answer: When Moses led the people of Israel to leave Egypt, God told His people: "When you go out to war against your enemies, and see horses and chariots, an army larger than your own, you shall not be afraid of them;

for the Lord your God is with you, who brought you up from the land of Egypt. …for it is the Lord your God who goes with you, to fight for you against your enemies, to give you victory'" (Deuteronomy 20:1-4).

When Joshua faced the enemies from Canaan, God commanded him, "Be strong and courageous; do not be frightened or dismayed, for the Lord your God is with you wherever you go." (Joshua 1:9) When God rescued David from being hunted by King Saul, David described his feeling of joy, gratitude, and praise in the Psalms. For example, in Psalms 18:32-40, David writes, "The God who girded me with strength, and made my way safe. He made my feet like the feet of a deer, and set me secure on the heights. He trains my hands for war, so that my arms can bend a bow of bronze. (v. 32-34)…You made my enemies turn their backs to me, and those who hated me I destroyed" (v. 40). Thus, Ezra's faith was built upon God's unbroken promise to His children throughout history.

❖Discussion and Sharing❖

(1) When your efforts are noticed and appreciated by your boss or superior, do you attribute the success to your own effort, or God's grace? Why?

Suggested answer: Before Jesus' light shone around him, Paul was a highly educated man and outstanding young leader. But after he knew God, he realized a truth and said,

"For who sees anything different in you? What do you have that you did not receive? And if you received it, why do you boast as if it were not a gift?" (1 Corinthians 4:7). Our wisdom and ability all come from God, and there is no reason for us to boast. God teaches us in Proverbs 11:2 that "when pride comes, then comes disgrace; but wisdom is with the humble." Again in Proverbs 16:18, we learn, "Pride goes before destruction, and a haughty spirit before a fall." In Matthew 5:3, Jesus says, "Blessed are the poor in spirit, for theirs is the kingdom of heaven."

If you take pride in yourself and steal God's credit, the consequences will be severe. In Acts 12, we observed how King Herod acted arrogantly and did not give glory to God. Immediately, "an angel of the Lord struck him down, and he was eaten by worms and died" (Acts 12:23). When we understand God's involvement in all things, we should properly attribute all good things to his commendation.

Even when we are frustrated, facing calamities as Job did, we can take courage because God is good and sovereign. As it says in James 5:11, "You have heard of the endurance of Job, and you have seen the purpose of the Lord, how the Lord is compassionate and merciful." We need to learn to "give thanks in all circumstances" (1 Thessalonians 5:18), because "we know that all things work together for good for those who love God, who are called according to his purpose." (Romans 8:28) Whether we are enjoying success or undergoing trials in our lives, we need to learn to give glory to the Lord in all things.

(2) From the text of Ezra 7, find the qualities of Ezra that made him a leader chosen by God.

Suggested answer: From Ezra 7:10-11, we know that Ezra had devoted himself to the study and observance of the Law of the Lord. Additionally, he did not just acquire the knowledge; he lived out its principles. His teaching of God's laws was effective because his words and behavior were consistent and compliant with the Lord's decrees. Besides, he was efficient (Ezra 7:6) and never delayed (Ezra 7:8-9). He was humble and did not claim credit for himself. He was certain that the hand of the Lord was on him and in everything he had done (Ezra 7: 27-28).

(3) Have you ever fasted and prayed? Please give examples of fasting and praying in the Bible. What do they mean to you?

Suggested answer: During the reign of Persian King Xerxes (Ahasuerus), the highest official Haman devised a scheme to have every Jew in Persia killed. When Queen Esther learned of the plot, she fasted and prayed. At the risk of her own life, she had to rescue her people. "Then Esther said in reply to Mordecai, 'Go, gather all the Jews to be found in Susa, and hold a fast on my behalf, and neither eat nor drink for three days, night or day. I and my maids will also fast as you do. After that I will go to the king, though it is against the law; and if I perish, I perish.'" (Esther 4:15-16) After their fasting and praying, God gave Esther wisdom and intervened in the situation, God saved all the Jews in despair.

From the passages in this lesson, we see that after Ezra's fasting and praying by the Ahava Canal (River Ahava), God's mighty hand led them safely to return to Jerusalem. "Then I proclaimed a fast there, at the River Ahava, that we might deny ourselves before our God, to seek from him a safe journey for ourselves, our children, and all our possessions. For I was ashamed to ask the king for a band of soldiers and cavalry to protect us against the enemy on our way, since we had told the king that the hand of our God is gracious to all who seek him, but his power and his wrath are against all who forsake him. So we fasted and petitioned our God for this, and he listened to our entreaty" (Ezra 8:21-23).

Jesus Christ gave us another example. After he was baptized, he was led by the Holy Spirit into the desert to be tempted by the devil, where he fasted forty days and forty nights. (See Matthew 4:1-2.) After Jesus was taken up to heaven, the apostles were filled by the Spirit and were emboldened to spread the gospel everywhere in order to establish churches. When they worshipped and fasted, the

Holy Spirit revealed to them the future direction, as described in Acts 13. "Now in the church at Antioch... While they were worshiping the Lord and fasting, the Holy Spirit said, 'Set apart for me Barnabas and Saul for the work to which I have called them.' Then after fasting and praying they laid their hands on them and sent them off" (Acts 13:1-3).

These examples show us that fasting and praying are essential practices to help Christians grow spiritually, serve vigorously, and walk in God's will wholeheartedly.

(4) When we answer God's calling and take a risk with a decision or project, how do we know God will accomplish His plan regardless of any obstacles?

Suggested answer: First and foremost, be certain about God's calling. It was a very difficult mission for Moses to lead the people of Israel out of Egypt; they would face danger in the wilderness, and threats from enemies. But Moses knew that God would protect them on the journey, because he was certain that the calling came from God. However, God's calling for everyone comes and works differently.

God's calling to Ezra was through the decree of King Artaxerxes, that he was to lead the Jews in Persia to return to Jerusalem for the second time without any delay. Although it would be a precarious journey, Ezra refused to ask the king for soldiers and horsemen to protect them on the road. Before their departure, he assembled all the returnees by the Ahava Canal to fast and petition God about their journey. From this instance, we understand that when we are taking risks with a decision or project, not only do we need to be certain the calling is from God, we also need to pray. We need to remember the importance of fasting and praying. The best way is to pray with partners together in front of God to seek His will and guidance.

Ezra 7:11 describes the priest Ezra as "the scribe, a scholar of the text of the commandments of the Lord and his statutes for Israel". The Bible provides God's revelation to His children and the assurance that we can understand God's will and ways. Therefore, to keep a habit of daily devotion to understand and obey His commands is an important way for us to seek God's protection when we embark on a new decision or project.

Finally, we have to honestly reflect on our motivation. In all the things we do, we do it so that we can give glory to God. If our calling is examined through praying and His revealed Word, and our motivation is to glorify God, we can be certain that God will lead us to accomplish His will even when it doesn't seem "successful." Even if the calling involves some amount of risk, we can be assured that God's will prevail, and God will guide us through.

Lesson 7: The Second Return Period (Part 2): Facing a Crisis of Faith; Restoration through Repentance and the Law (Ezra 9:1-10:44)

Suggested answers for your reference:

❖Fill in the blanks❖

(1) "The people of Israel, the priests, and the Levites have not separated themselves from the peoples of the lands with their abominations, from the (Canaanites), the Hittites, the Perizzites, the (Jebusites), the Ammonites, the (Moabites), the Egyptians, and the Amorites. For they have taken some of their daughters as wives for themselves and for their sons. Thus the holy seed has mixed itself with the peoples of the lands, and in this faithlessness the (officials) and (leaders) have led the way" (Ezra 9:1-2).

(2) "O Lord, God of Israel, you are (just), but we have escaped as a remnant, as is now the case. Here we are before you in our (guilt), though no one can face you because of this" (Ezra 9:15).

(3) "Then (Ezra) the priest stood up and said to them, 'You have trespassed and married (foreign women), and so increased the guilt of Israel" (Ezra 10:10).

(4) There was a clay tablet in the Louvre related to "Shevat". It shows that during captivity, the Jews were influenced by

the local culture and had adopted the (Babylonian) calendar.

❖Scripture study❖

(1) What is the name of the prophet who served the returnees in Jerusalem at about the same time as Ezra? What did he have to say about marrying foreign women?

Suggested answer: The prophet Malachi lived during the same time period as Ezra. They both served the returned exiles. Through Malachi, God revealed His abomination about marrying foreign women. (cf. Malachi 2:10-16)

(2) "When I heard this, I tore my garment and my mantle, and pulled hair from my head and beard, and sat appalled." (Ezra 9:3). In the Old and New Testament, can you find out other examples of similar behavior?

Suggested answer: To tear one's tunic and cloak or to cover one's hair and garments with ashes were common ways for kings or common people of Israel to express their shock or grief. We can find a similar description in the following passages: Genesis 37:29, 34; Joshua 7:6; Job 1:20; Isaiah 36:22; Esther 4:1; Matthew 26:65.

(3) In the practice of Babylonians, following a divorce, children left with their mothers. Are there similar examples in the Bible?

Suggested Answers

Suggested answer: According to the Bible, after a divorce, the child of the divorced parents left with the mother and moved away from the father. The earliest mention of such a custom was seen in Genesis 21:14: in his obedience to God's command and submitting to Sarah's request, Abraham sent Hagar and Ishmael away from his household.

❖Discussion and Sharing❖

(1) Is there a crisis of faith within marriage today?

Suggested answer: When we don't understand God's words fully, we will likely follow the crowd, and drift along with the current. Christians today face several challenges to their faith in marriages. Because Christians make up only a small portion of the entire population, sometimes we may be pressured to consider marrying non-Christians. Christians can befriend non-believers and share our beliefs with others. However, before entering the courtship, we must carefully seek God's guidance, and not to be led by our own affection and desire of the flesh.

In addition, Christian marriages of today also face the challenge of same-sex marriage. The world might advocate for same-sex marriage from the perspectives of psychology or human rights, however, Jesus was very clear in addressing and defining marriage in Matthew 19:4-6. "He answered, "Have you not read that the one who made them at the beginning 'made them male and female,' and said, 'For this reason a man shall leave his father and mother and be joined to his wife, and the two shall become one flesh'? So they are no longer two, but one flesh. Therefore, what God has joined together, let no one separate." referencing both Genesis 1:26-27 and Genesis 2:24. (Also see Mark 10:6-9.) Jesus affirmed marriage as between a man and a woman, reflecting that God made us male and female to order creation together. With this definition, same-sex marriage is excluded from Christian obedience. Let us trust God's good design for marriage, and consider with careful consideration His coming judgment. As stated in Hebrews 13:4, "Let marriage be held in honor by all, and let the marriage bed be kept undefiled; for God will judge fornicators and adulterers."

To deal with the crisis of faith that Christians face today, we need the wisdom and guidance of the Holy Spirit, as well as a full understanding of God's love and firm standing in the assurance of salvation through Christ's accepted sacrifice in exchange of sin for righteousness.

(2) When we see our brothers and sisters trapped in sins, what can we learn from Ezra's actions?
Suggested answer: Ezra was so bitterly grieved by his fellow countrymen that he pulled the hair from his head and

beard, mourned, and prayed for them. Then he led them to pray and confess their sin. When they all repented for their sins, he listed out the steps that they needed to take, made sure that their repentance was truthful, and that going forward they would live according to God's will. We can learn from and follow every step of his approach.

(3) When we see Christian brothers and sisters dating a person not yet a Christian, what can we say to them?

Suggested answer: We can say to them that different faiths between a husband and wife reveal the differences in their value systems, and a difference in priorities and decision-making in their daily lives. Dr. John Piper once said, "Marriage is a union of the deepest kind; it's meant to be a union of soul, as well as a union of body. There can't be any deep union of soul if two people have different supreme treasures." Too many differences between the couple will strain their relationship and their intimacy and trust will gradually be exhausted. In the case of the Samaritans, we learned that they choose to compromise, and eventually drifted away from their original faith. That is why it is said in 2 Corinthians 6:14, "Do not be mismatched with unbelievers." This is not God's unloving command, but God's protection for His children lest we lose the blessings that God wants to bestow on our marriage.

Appendix

Spring of Water International Ministry
Multimedia Bible Learning Material
Instruction for Small Group Leaders and
Teachers

The term "the group leader" below is referred to anyone who is leading the Bible study group.

The Bible Study Process of *SOW* Multimedia Bible Learning Materials (SMBLM)

Following an "open learning" principle and the Bible study course scheduling in general, SMBLM allows 50-120 minutes for each lesson of the study guide. Every lesson has three stages: Preparation, Development, and Conclusion, with allocated time of 5-15 minutes, 40-90 minutes, and 5-15 minutes, respectively. The group leader can adjust the time periods and course content to fit the needs of the situation. SMBLM can also be adopted in a class-room Bible- teaching process. Each stage is described in detail below:

A. Preparation (5-15 minutes):

The purpose of this stage is to warm up the Bible study group members, lead them into the direction of the lesson, and spark their interest in learning. Depending on the time available and the occasion, the group leader can conduct any of the following activities:

1. Ice-breaker: While waiting for late arrivals, ice-breaker activities can be conducted in any of the following ways:

    A. Introduce new comers.

    B. Greet one another by asking a question.

    C. Share what is happening around each person, or any application from the previous lesson, or any development on things that we are praying through in our intercessory prayers.

    D. Discuss the latest news or events of interest to all.

    E. Play a game related to the subject of study of the day.

2. Introduction: Introduce the subject of the lesson and give a mental sketch for the direction of the study. It can be conducted in one of the following ways:

A. Introduce the goals of the lesson.

B. Present the outline of the lesson.

C. Sum up what was taught in the previous lesson, then begin the subject of the lesson.

D. Ask a question that is relevant to the lesson of the day and allow the group members to answer, then proceed into the subject.

3. Opening Prayer: Before going into the subject of the lesson, pray and read the Scriptures to prepare our hearts to learn and be humble.

A. Pray for the presence of the Holy Spirit that will anoint the words of the group leader, and open the hearts of the group members, to let in Christ Jesus' living water as the creek of learning for the class, that nurtures and enriches everyone.

B. Read aloud the **key** verses that lead to the study subject of the lesson.

B. Development (40-90 minutes):

This stage is where the main activities of SMBLM Bible study are organized. The focus is to have group members assimilate new learning into their existing cognitive system effectively through a multi-faceted and fun-filled process.

The group leader can conduct the Development stage in the following manner:

I. Scripture Reading: Everyone takes turn reading aloud or in silence the portion of the Scriptures as described in the course schedule, to establish the outline.

II. Synopsis: The group leader should give a brief summary for about 3 to 10 minutes about the text, or through questions and answers in Scripture study to bring out the main points and help group members to recall, digest, and consolidate what they learned.

III. Video Viewing: Play the video clip as suggested for the lesson. Most sessions will last about 5 to 10 minutes. Make sure to have a suitable environment by keeping things such as light, volume, and noises in check.

IV. Study Questions: Group participation is essential here in this phase. The group leader leads the Bible study group members to discuss, share, or apply items that are within the scope of the lesson. During such activity, interaction among group members should take the majority of the time, and the group leader should only be the role of a facilitator. It is recommended not to exceed 30% of the total time by the group leader. At the end, the group leader will move to the next phase of concluding the discussion, moderating sharing, and suggest any application from the lesson.

C. Conclusion (5-15 minutes):

The purpose is to consolidate the lessons learned through the study, and lead the group members to apply them in their daily lives.

1. Summary: At the end of each study, the group leader gives a review of what has been learned, to make sure each group member has clear understanding of the Scripture and reaches the goals of the lesson. It can be conducted in any of the following ways:

    A. Review the lesson.

    B. Assess the effectiveness of the study through questions and answers.

    C. Apply today's lesson and anticipate future learning.

D. Read aloud together the **key** Bible verses related to the study.

E. Encourage group members to practice what they just learned in their daily living.

2. Closing Prayer: For a large group, the group leader can be the one who prays for the whole group and conclude the study. For a smaller group, it can be done through intercessory prayers among the group members. Praying for each other is not only a spiritual practice, but it also develops and grows relationships among group members.

SMBLM uses the multimedia materials as a platform, and allows Bible study group leaders to be the facilitator of discussion and sharing. The following table is a lesson plan of using SMBLM to lead a Bible study group or to be adopted in a Sunday school class:

Table 1: Multimedia Bible Teaching Materials Teaching Procedures	
I. Preparation (5-15 minutes)	
1	Ice-breaker
2	Introduction
3	Opening Prayer
II. Development (40-90 minutes)	
1	Scripture Reading
2	Synopsis
3	Video Viewing
4	Study Questions
III. Conclusion (5-15 minutes)	
1	Summary, Homework Assignment
2	Closing Prayer